Some Party In Heaven

NOEL I. DAVIDSON

AMBASSADOR

Some Party In Heaven
First published 1995
Copyright © Noel Davidson

ISBN 1 898787 53 0

Ambassador Productions Ltd.
Providence House
16 Hillview Avenue,
Belfast, BT5 6JR
Northern Ireland

• • •

Emerald House
1 Chick Springs Road, Suite 102
Greenville,
South Carolina 29609

Contents

✤ ✤ ✤

DEDICATION

This book is dedicated to Ford and Matthew
and the memory of Thomas and Wendsley

Introduction

✤ ❖ ✤

"I really love a sad story," a lady remarked recently. "When I have read one and have had a good cry I feel great."

What gives you that 'feel-good factor'? That sense of well-being which we experience, unfortunately, all too seldom.

Do you like a sad story? Or 'a good cry'?

A friend told me the story of Hertford and Phyllis Arnold about a year ago. It was a sad story. Tragic, indeed.

But it didn't make me feel good. The very opposite, in fact. It made me feel miserable.

How could that young couple survive the recurring traumas of their experience? It seemed impossible.

Then something happened that changed my whole perspective. I met Hertford and Phyllis.

As we sat together after a meal, Phyllis produced a photograph album and wept freely as she told of one thing after another.

Yet it wasn't all doom and gloom.

A sparkle could be seen in a tear-clouded eye.

"Oh, I'm sure you think I'm making an awful fool of myself," she apologised, "but we are so delighted that someone is interested in telling our story. You see we believe that these things happened to bring us to God and to strengthen our faith in Him. If a book is written about our lives we would want all the glory and praise to go to God, Who has brought us through this far."

I undertook to write their story, to give praise to God, and started into a regular research pattern ...

However, as we sat together that June evening of our first meeting, none of us had any idea of the perfect ending God had planned. The turn of events that was about to occur in the lives of that young couple could never have entered our heads ...

As you read this story you may have 'a good cry'. And that may even make you 'feel good'.

But if you read this book and come into a deeper and fuller relationship with our loving, caring God, it will make you feel infinitely better.

May God make it a blessing to you.

Noel I. Davidson
1995

Other books by the same author:-

My Father's Hand
This Is For Real
Just The Way I Am.

Proceeds from the sale of this book will be used to further Christ's Kingdom at home and abroad
---

CHAPTER ONE

Will You Go?

✤ ✤ ✤

"If the Lord Jesus was to come right now, I wonder how many from this room would rise to meet Him?"

The voice of Hedley Murphy challenged the audience in a meeting in Moira, Co. Down. The atmosphere was solemn. Silent and still.

Young Phyllis Blakely glanced from side to side. She was almost seventeen years old. Her mother had persuaded her to go to the meeting, with her sister Gloria.

"It would really please your uncle Eddie," she had coaxed.

As she observed those seated around her, Phyllis came to the conclusion that most of them would "rise to meet Jesus" if He was to come that moment. She knew them. Fine, Christian, meeting-going types the majority of them. They were all people of high moral standard and well-spoken of in the countryside.

Yes. They would mostly all rise.

Then there was Gloria, sitting beside her. Gloria was a good girl. Clean living, decent sort of person, perhaps a Christian, so she would probably go too.

That just left herself. When she came to close self-scrutiny, the arrow of conviction embedded itself deep into her heart.

If the Lord Jesus was to come tonight, she wouldn't rise to meet Him.

It was as simple as that.

She wasn't ready.

She wasn't saved.

And she knew that perfectly well.

That knowledge made her determined. This was going to be the night. Phyllis was going to settle the matter, once and for all. And it was going to be tonight.

Sitting there, she gradually lost all sense of her surroundings. She drifted into reverie.

Thoughts flooded back into her troubled mind.

Phyllis remembered the messages that she had heard as a little child, in the Kilmore Gospel Hall. That, in turn, made her think of the McCanns. How faithful they had been, collecting her every Sunday to take her to Sunday School.

Genuine Christians the McCanns.

They would go when Jesus came. No doubt about that.

Still the verses, choruses and snippets of Bible stories continued to zip out of her memory bank to bombard her whirling brain.

Reminiscence returned rapidly to reality, however, when the preacher's voice announced the final hymn.

"Let's sing in closing ..." he was saying,

"When the trumpet of the Lord shall sound."

The congregation creaked stiffly into standing mode and began to sing lustily.

They seemed to sing with particular conviction the last line of each verse, repeated in the chorus,

"When the roll is called up yonder, I'll be there."

Phyllis didn't sing. She just prayed, inwardly, earnestly.

She was broken. Tears trickled silently down her cheeks.

"Lord, please don't come yet," she pleaded. "These people all believe they are going to be "there". I want to be "there" too. O Lord, please don't come until I get saved!"

As the congregation filed out, Phyllis hung back. She wanted to speak to the preacher. She need help. Tonight was the night. Tuesday, 17th February, 1981. This was it.

Mr. Hedley Murphy spoke to her gently. He read verses from the Bible. Many of them she recognised, having committed them to memory in Kilmore Gospel Hall Sunday School.

Then she prayed. It was a sincere prayer from the heart.

"Lord Jesus," she began, "I know that I am a sinner. I need You to save and change me. I believe that You died on the cross to take away my sins. As I come to You now, please forgive my sin and make me Your own."

With that the burden of sin disappeared. There came a realization that she was saved.

It had been so simple to trust in Jesus.

A tremendous sense of peace enfolded her.

Phyllis just wished that she could relive the end of the meeting so that she could sing with God-fearing gusto, along with all the others, "When the roll is called up yonder I'll be there."

As she left the room, uncle Eddie was waiting. He hadn't gone home. Stepping towards her, and interpreting her smile as a happy harbinger, he said, "Well, Phyllis ...?" Half a statement, more a question.

Phyllis was radiant and confident, by now.

"I got saved tonight, uncle Eddie," she blurted out.

"Oh that's great!" Eddie Weir made no attempt whatsoever to conceal his delight.

"That's an answer to prayer. I have been praying that one of you Blakelys would soon get saved."

Phyllis was only one of the Blakelys. There were seven of them. Besides Gloria who had come with her there were Heather, Alva, Jackson, Estlin, and Linden.

Most of these others had been asked to come, but they all with one consent began to make excuse.

"I have to fix my car," claimed one.

"I have to see my girl-friend," said another.

"I've arranged to meet one of my mates in Lurgan at half seven," was a third excuse. So it went on.

But Phyllis and Gloria had gone. To please either mother or uncle Eddie, or both.

Now Phyllis was saved, and this pleased them both.

When her mother heard of the night's big event, she too rejoiced.

Her pleasure was less exuberant, more self-controlled, than that of her uncle Eddie, but genuine, nonetheless.

"You have made the right decision, Phyllis," she assured her daughter. "May God bless you."

News travels fast when it is good. By the time she arrived home from the meeting, her dad knew as well!

He stopped his radiant daughter as they met in the kitchen doorway. "You will never regret the decision you made to-night, Phyllis," were his simple words of encouragement.

Next morning, at breakfast, however, Phyllis began to think that her mother had changed her mind.

She began to probe, to question.

"Are you sure, Phyllis, that it wasn't just your emotions that overcame you last night?" she enquired.

Mothers know their daughters through and through. Ethel Blakely was no exception. She knew her Phyllis. She was an emotional girl, easily touched. Phyllis would be liable to react spontaneously in a highly-charged atmosphere.

"No, mother. This is no emotional thing. This is the real thing. I got saved last night. I got Jesus in my heart last night."

Mother was convinced. When she heard the new convert's calm declaration in the cold clear light of a new day, she was satisfied.

Her daughter would need some advice now, she knew.

"You will find, Phyllis," she began, softly, "that the things that once interested you won't interest you as much any more. And you will probably find, too, that your old friends won't want you so much, either. But don't let that worry you. You have found the Saviour, and that is the most important thing in life. You will soon find new friends, with the same desires as yourself."

With that sensible counsel ringing in her ears, Phyllis set off for work.

When she arrived home in the evening Phyllis found that the 'New Christians Advice Bureau' was ready to begin another session. With mother as adviser-in-chief.

The local Christian community was abuzz with the news. Family, friends and relations had been on the phone to Mrs. Blakely.

"Great to hear about Phyllis," they had said with one accord.

Then came the variety of advice ...

"Tell her to seek out Christian friends," they said.

"Tell her to read the Bible every day," they said.

"Make sure she doesn't neglect her prayer times," they said.

Uncle Eddie's advice summarised them all.

"Eric Spence runs a prayer meeting and Bible study in his home in Hillsborough every Wednesday evening. It would be a good idea if she could start going there," he suggested.

When Ethel Blakely told Phyllis of all those who had been ringing she was pleased. She hadn't really been aware that so many people could be so genuinely concerned about her.

After recounting all the recommendations she had recorded, mother finished up with uncle Eddie's advice about the prayer meeting.

"Will you go, Phyllis?" she asked, in conclusion.

Phyllis didn't hesitate. Now that she was prepared to go to meet Jesus when He came, she could probably manage to make it to a prayer meeting in Hillsborough, she reckoned.

"Of course I'll go, mother!" was her immediate answer. "I'll start next week!"

And she did.

Her brother Alva's girlfriend, Marjorie, bought her a little book. It was called "Sunrise to Sunset", - a book of daily readings by Derick Bingham. Phyllis was really blessed by that book.

So eager was she to learn more about her newly-found faith that she read the book from "sunrise to sunset", and half the night as well!

Gradually the babe-in-Christ began to show signs of growth. The desire for Scripture reading, prayer meetings and all things spiritual was increasing.

Phyllis couldn't understand it all herself. Before that hallowed night in Moira, she used to think that Christians were a crowd of stiff stooges, stuffed shirts, wet blankets. Now that she was one of them herself, she realised that they were none of these things.

At least she wasn't anyway!

It was great!

Going to and from the Wednesday evening prayer meeting, and many another time besides, Phyllis listened to a tape which someone had given to her.

It was of hymns, sung by Rev. William McCrea.

As the little brown Mini, which her dad had bought her for her seventeenth birthday, sped on its way, it reverberated to the strains of "Worthy is the Lamb", "Will the Circle be Unbroken?" and other well known hymns. Often, Rev. McCrea had the accompaniment of Phyllis as she sang along, beating out time on the steering wheel!

Phyllis felt so close to the Saviour on those occasions that she used to commune with Him, as she travelled along.

"Lord, I just feel You sitting there beside me," she would say, in hushed tones. "I can't see You I know, but I can feel You so close to me. Thank you. Thank You. Thank You, Lord!"

CHAPTER TWO

You Are Mine, Aren't You?

✤ ✤ ✤

The Arnold brothers, Hertford and Tyrrell, were interested in fast cars. They spent most of their spare time either racing their cars or taking them to bits and putting them together again. All in an attempt to coax a few more miles-per-hour out of well-worn engines.

The Blakely brothers, Jackson and Estlin, also spent a high percentage of their leisure time in following motor-sport. This mutual interest led to a bond of friendship developing between Hertford and Tyrrell, the road racers, and the Blakely fast car enthusiasts. They all attended the race meetings together, though some of them possibly enjoyed the social side of the sport as much as they did the thrills and spills of the track. Discussing the performance of the cars over a few beers in a bar was as satisfying to them as hearing the deafening roar of the engines and the squeal of tortured, smoking rubber.

Hertford's interest in cars, and in tinkering with them, led to him becoming a frequent visitor to the Blakely home.

After a few months, Jackson and Estlin began to suspect that their friend was interested in more than revs-per-minute. Something was happening to his own heartbeat, they reckoned. But they said nothing. Time would tell.

They were to be proved correct. Hertford was beginning to cast admiring glances toward their sister, Phyllis. He wasn't hard to persuade to slide out from in below an engine, and put the spanner down, when she came out into the yard to chat to all the lads.

One night, just before he left for home, Hertford dashed into the kitchen where Phyllis was, and said, "I would like to take you out some night next week, Phyllis, if that's O.K. Any night you like."

Her two brothers, who had been brushed aside, then totally ignored, as Hertford made his first date with Phyllis, nodded and winked at each other. They knew this would happen. They had seen it coming for weeks.

Phyllis pretended to look amazed.

Then she looked really pleased.

An uncontrollable blush glowed on her cheek.

"That would be nice," she replied, shyly.

Unknown to him, she had rather fancied this strong, frank and friendly fellow who seemed to be coming about their household more and more. The most trivial matter seemed to have given him an excuse to call round.

Now she knew why! But she wasn't complaining!

So it was arranged. They went out together on the following Wednesday night, and enjoyed it. Something "clicked". They found they liked each other, and had some common interests.

The next step was to meet again. And they did, on the following Wednesday night.

Thus it went on.

A pattern became established. Every Wednesday night and most Saturday nights, they met.

There was only one difficulty though. This single complication highlighted a particular area where Hertford, and his new girl-friend, Phyllis, did not have a common interest.

Wednesday was Bible study and prayer meeting night. As Phyllis began to fall in love with Hertford, she began to cool down towards the Lord.

When the racing season went over, and autumn days grew shorter, the young couple began to spend more time in the pubs and at the dances than beside the track.

Phyllis never felt at ease in these places. She was happy in Hertford's company.

Yes, increasingly so.

She wasn't happy in the haunts where she often found herself, just to be in his company.

No, increasingly no.

"This is not right!" her spiritual conscience claimed with alarming frequency, as she heard the name of her Lord being taken in vain. "You shouldn't be here!"

When she mentioned it to Hertford, he just laughed at her.

"Can we not just go for a drive or a walk, or sit in and watch T.V. or something?" she would ask every now and again. "I don't like the crowd in those pubs we go to. I'm saved you know."

"What do you mean, you're 'saved'?" he would jibe. "You were always a decent-living girl Phyllis. You don't need all that kind of stuff. Neither do I, for that matter."

Thus Phyllis became the centre of a spiritual tug-of-war.

On one side, it appeared, grabbing one wrist, holding tightly, and pulling hard was Hertford, whom she loved dearly.

"I love you, Phyllis. You are mine," he was saying.

On the opposite side, holding the other wrist, and pulling gently but firmly was her Lord, whom she also loved dearly.

"I loved you so much that I died for you, Phyllis. You are mine," He was saying.

Phyllis was sure that she was going to be spiritually pulled in two. There was always this constant contest.

Hertford versus the Lord.

The Lord versus Hertford.

Gradually the winner emerged.

Phyllis had stopped attending her weekly Bible study when she met Hertford. Now her personal Bible study was becoming more erratic.

Regular precious prayer times gave place to hurried shopping-lists to God when things weren't going too great.

Rev. William McCrea was tucked away, unheard, into a side pocket of the Mini. There the once-upon-a-time popular tape kept company with a duster, a dried up chamois, and a can of de-icer with a cracked cap.

They had just been 'going out' with each other for seven weeks when Hertford made a sudden proposal one Saturday evening.

The evening had gone well, and the warmth of the love that was shared between them was becoming more evident. This was the right time for the big one, he was sure.

"Phyllis, I love you and I want to marry you," he stated quite simply. "How about us getting engaged at Christmas?"

She just couldn't believe it! Phyllis was pleased and thrilled, stunned and speechless all at once. Surely this was only the drink talking. Hertford had taken a pint of two that evening.

When she reined in her runaway thoughts, she expressed the doubts that clouded her delight, to her would-be husband.

"You don't really mean it, Hertford," she began. "You don't know what you're talking about! Sure we have only been going with each other for six or seven weeks!"

"I do know what I'm talking about! And I do mean it!" was Hertford's instinctive reply.

Phyllis needed time. She just had to think this whole matter through.

"O.K. Hertford, O.K. I believe you," she conceded. "But this is important you know. I need time to think about it. You have sprung this all on me so suddenly! Ask me tomorrow night, and I'll tell you!"

Hertford Arnold was a young man of purpose. He liked instant answers and immediate action. No hanging about or messing around.

Waiting wasn't a thing he was very good at.

He agreed, reluctantly.

"Right," he declared. "I will be here tomorrow night at eight o'clock. Will you be able to answer me then?"

"I will, I promise," Phyllis assured him.

With that, they kissed, and parted.

As soon as she got into the house, Phyllis rushed up to her bedroom. Throwing off her coat, and kicking off her shoes, she launched herself across the bed. She landed in a half prostrate, half-praying position, and there she remained.

"Lord," she prayed in turmoil, "if Hertford Arnold is the man for me, please let me know. And if he's not, drive him away from me, somehow. Lord, please show me what to do. I need to know Your will for me, Lord. And I need to know it before eight o'clock tomorrow night!"

Still there was the struggle.

Trying to please the Lord, and love Hertford.

Now he had gone and complicated the whole issue even further by asking her to marry him!

Sunday seemed unending.

For Phyllis it was a trying-to-make-your-mind-up kind of day.

Gazing out the window, she wondered, "What will I do?"

Picking at her meals, she wondered, "What should I say?"

Barely a single word of the general babbling of the busy Blakely household blethering registered with her, as she wondered, "What am I going to tell him?"

As the day progressed, the answer came. She began to listen to her heart. Just as the early morning mist burns away with the heat of the sun, slowly revealing the surrounding landscape, so the picture became clearer, bit by bit.

When Hertford drove into the yard, spot on eight o'clock, in his father's grey Granada, Phyllis was waiting. She hopped in beside him.

"Well, what's your answer to what I asked you last night?" was Hertford's immediate question. There was no, "You're looking well tonight, love," or "Nice night, isn't it?"

Direct as ever, her impatient boyfriend came straight to the point.

"You remember, Phyllis, I asked you last night would you marry me? You promised me you would tell me tonight. Well, I'm waiting ... what's your answer?"

Hertford switched off the engine, very deliberately. They weren't going anywhere else or doing anything else, until he knew.

Phyllis threw herself across into his arms.

"Yes! Yes! Yes!" she replied, repeatedly.

The young couple hugged each other in ecstasy. They believed now that they were meant for each other.

"There's just one wee problem, though," Phyllis brought them both back down to earth, when she regained her breath.

A fleeting shadow crossed Hertford's face. He was worried, but only slightly, and only momentarily.

"What's your wee problem?" he enquired.

"I think Christmas would be too soon to get engaged," she explained.

"Daddy would have a fit if we ever mentioned it. Could we leave it off for a bit? Say, to my birthday?"

Hertford agreed to that. After all, her birthday, he knew, was only a little over two months after Christmas.

So, just to emphasise the genuine nature of his intentions, Hertford brought Phyllis a gold watch for Christmas.

The engagement ring came for her eighteenth birthday, on 7th March, 1982.

CHAPTER THREE

Happy Days

✤✤✤

The wedding of Hertford and Phyllis on 23rd April, 1983, in High Street Presbyterian Church, Lurgan, was a happy occasion.

In addition to the joining together of two loving hearts, it afforded an opportunity for a coming together of two large families.

As wedding days so often are for parents, it was a day of joy, tinged with just a hint of sadness for Tom and Ethel Blakely and Ford and Jean Arnold. They were pleased at the prospects for their children, but conscious of a gap looming up ahead somewhere for themselves.

Brothers and sisters of both bride and groom assisted in every possible way to make the 'big day' a success. Some were in the bridal party, others acted as ushers at the church, and all the remainder attended with their husbands or wives, boyfriends or girlfriends, contributing much to the overall happiness of the event.

Everyone enjoyed themselves, basking in the warmth of the infectious love of Hertford and Phyllis.

After the wedding, the young couple moved into the Arnold family home. Hertford's parents had built a new house, leaving theirs for the newly-weds.

It was a good house, a solid country house.

The main feature of their new abode was the massive kitchen with its great terrazzo floor, white Aga, and huge twelve foot by five foot table.

This gigantic table, their dominant item of furniture, proved to be the setting for some heart-to-heart conversations between the young couple.

Hertford sat at one end of the long table.

His new wife was seated just around the corner, beside him.

Often, when a meal was finished they would push the empty plates away from them and look at one another, then up at the length of the table. They would ponder, and dream, and chat.

Mostly, though, the theme of their conversation was the same every time.

It was about a family. Their family. The family that they hoped so much that they were going to have.

"How long do you think it will be until we have a family big enough to fill every chair?" would come the question.

"Ten or twelve years, likely, unless we have a set or two of twins!" would come the reply.

"How many boys do you think there will be?"

"How many girls?"

Thus the question and answer fantasy sessions continued, fuelled by much love and punctuated by much laughter.

These end-of-the-table, end-of-a-meal, affectionate exchanges reflected an ambition of both husband and wife.

They had both come from large, and happy families.

They would both like to have a large, and happy, family.

Both of them were overjoyed, then, a few months later, when Phyllis found out that she was expecting a baby. Their dream had taken at least its first tiny step toward fulfilment.

During those days of early married life, Phyllis was vaguely conscious of God. She used to pray to Him, but only sometimes, and usually only when something was troubling her.

She had lost her Christian conscience also. Things that once caused raging storms of guilt to buffet her burdened soul didn't even create the faintest ripple now.

Anyway, she had something else to occupy her mind. There was someone else to talk about, to plan for. Her Saviour was shoved back into a distant third place in the race for her priority thinking.

Sitting side by side before the Aga on many an evening, often with the lower oven door open and their feet jammed into it for heat, Hertford and she would discuss the baby-to-come.

"What room should we do up for him or her?" was one topic of discussion. Other matters considered at some length ranged from prams and cots to toys and nappies.

Everything for little junior was going to be of the very best they could afford.

It was so important to them.

They were ever so content.

Just one thing Hertford didn't like. It was being left on his own, at work on the farm, when Phyllis attended her antenatal clinic. Time dragged when she was away.

On her return, her anxious husband was invariably waiting in the yard.

In his own direct, but caring manner, he would enquire, "Well, how are you today? What had the doctor to say about the both of you?"

Then they would go into the house, put the kettle on the Aga, and Phyllis would give him a detailed, word-by-word account of what the doctor had said about her condition.

When he was satisfied that everybody concerned was fit and well, and Phyllis kept assuring him that the doctor had told her that they were, then Hertford would return to work. That was usually half-an-hour and two cups of coffee later!

Christmas, 1983, was a joyful time for the young couple. It was their first Christmas together.

As she decorated the tree in the corner of the living room, Phyllis remarked to her devoted husband, "Just think, Hertford. Next Christmas there will be three of us. We will have a baby to share all this with!"

On New Year's Day, 1984, a Sunday, Phyllis had lunch with Hertford's parents. In the afternoon she was admitted to Lagan Valley Hospital, Lisburn.

Again, Phyllis found herself coping with that mixed-feeling sensation. She didn't really relish the prospect of giving birth to her first-born, but she did look forward to having her very own baby to nurse.

As she lay in her hospital bed she prayed about it. Although the fire of her faith had long since faded to a flicker, she communed with her Lord about what lay ahead.

"Lord, please help me in the coming days," she would pray, and always there was the same conclusion, the final request.

"And please, Lord, let the baby be born safely."

On Thursday, 5th January 1984 her prayers were answered.

Thomas Jackson Arnold was born, called after his Granda Blakely.

He was some baby, too, tipping the scales at eleven pounds, seven and a half ounces!

The news spread like wildfire through the maternity unit. Some of the workers from the canteen visited the ward as they went off duty.

"We just called in to see this big fellow, so that we can measure him up for his school uniform!" they joked.

The interest of the hospital staff, however, didn't in any way match the delight of his mother and father.

They were parents now, and proud of it!

Hertford rang everybody whom he thought would be even remotely interested. He was so thrilled!

The family circle on both sides were overjoyed as well. Everyone loved the young couple, and they all knew of their desire for a sizeable family.

Thomas was a sturdy start to their campaign.

Phyllis, the radiant mother, just glowed.

When she wasn't actually nursing the baby out of the cot, she was watching him in it, or rearranging the rapidly increasing collection of flowers, toys and teddies around it.

On the day when she was told that she could go home, it snowed, heavily.

Phyllis phoned Hertford.

"We can go home, Hertford!" she exclaimed, excitedly. "Can you come for me? What are the roads like? Even if you have to hire a helicopter, can you bring us home?"

Hertford's days in motor-sport hadn't been wasted after all. He knew a trick or two about driving in all conditions. A foot of snow wouldn't deter him from getting his wife and infant son home!

"Don't you worry about a thing, Phyllis," was his definite reply. "If they are going to let you home, we will surely get you home!"

Phyllis loved her husband's determination. She was pleased with his decision. Above everything else, she wanted to be back at home with her husband and their little baby boy.

Tyrrell came with Hertford, and they made it to the Hospital though the roads were well covered with snow.

What an exciting home coming!

Driving back up the M1 through deep snow, in the red Escort XR3, Tyrrell had a big responsibility. The conditions were bad and the cargo was precious.

Phyllis nursed baby Thomas.

Hertford's attention was divided. It was a three-way split. He was either concentrating on the hazardous conditions outside, his wife, now a mother, or their little baby son.

Before leaving for the Hospital, Hertford had stoked up the fire. And what a fire!

The living room was like an oven when they entered it. The tiles on the hearth were too hot to touch, and the chimney breast creaked in agony.

It was bitter winter weather, and his wife and son weren't going to be starved in a cold house!

The warmth of their arrival was to herald happy days to come.

The resounding echo had gone from the kitchen now.

Nappies, a baby bath, a carry cot and sterilizing units were the additional essential items of equipment. Objects of various sizes, shapes and colours that either shook, rattled or squeaked were the ornaments.

The big table always had something sitting on it.

Hertford remarked once that it took more space for baby Thomas, with all his bits and pieces, "and all the size of him too," than it did for Phyllis and he put together!

A new member of the Arnold household had come home.

Things were never going to be quite the same again!

CHAPTER FOUR

Oh No!

✦✦✦

Baby Thomas brought much delight to many. He was the centre of attention in the family circle.

The whole lifestyle of his young parents was readjusted to accommodate his needs. Programmes of work, snatched moments of leisure, and even the extent of any night's sleep were geared to fit in with his eating, sleeping, waking and resting patterns.

It was quite a change for Hertford, who once believed that you worked hard by day and slept soundly at night, to be standing perched on one leg by the Aga, at two o'clock in the morning, heating a bottle. The other foot was being kept warm in the bottom oven. A terrazzo floor was desperately cold on the bare feet!

His grandparents on both sides and his new aunts and uncles kept calling at the house, or ringing up, to enquire about Thomas.

"Well, how's the big man today?" they would ask.

Phyllis' sister Heather, however, had a particular interest in babies in general, and two in particular, at that time. She had just had a baby herself, a girl with a shock of jet black hair, called Carolyn.

As Carolyn was her second child, Heather felt herself qualified by experience to help and advise Phyllis, a novice, on matters relating to the care of her infant son.

One afternoon in mid-March 1984, Phyllis went round to Heather's house in Dromore for a chat. As always she had Thomas with her in his carry-cot.

Hertford was busy in the fields, preparing to sow the barley. It was a pleasant, warming-up type of an early Spring day. The firs t of the daffodils were beginning to reveal just a hint of yellow. It was the sort of an afternoon in which the dark days of winter faded from the memory. There was life in the air. And hope.

The two mothers and sisters sat in Heather's kitchen and fed their babies. They chatted animatedly to one another as the bottles were emptied.

Something Phyllis noticed though caused her just a speck of concern. She had observed it before but hadn't mentioned it to anyone.

Thomas was always slow to finish his bottles. Carolyn was a month younger, but usually had hers scoffed in half the time.

As Heather placed the empty bottle on the table, and straightened her baby up "to get up her wind," Phyllis remarked, "She couldn't have finished already!"

'She couldn't.' But she had!

When the feeding session was over, Phyllis and Heather went into the living room for a leisurely gossip. They would allow their babies to lie on the floor and stretch and kick.

It would be a refreshing time for all of them.

Heather was on her knees on the floor, adjusting the changing mats, and making sure the children were comfortable. Her back was to Phyllis, who was sitting back in a corner of the settee.

Tying to sound as casual as possible, Phyllis asked the question which had begun to niggle her.

"Heather, do you not notice a difference between Thomas and Carolyn?"

Heather didn't turn around, didn't look up.

She just answered, "What do you mean, Phyllis?"

Before explaining exactly what it was that she meant, Phyllis stood up. Then, looking tenderly down at her cherished Thomas as he lay flat on the floor, she blurted it out.

"Do you not think there is something wrong with him, Heather?" she asked quickly. The words seemed to explode from her mouth like fizz from a much shaken drink can. She had to get it over with.

Now it was out. What would be the reaction?

Nothing at first.

There was an awkward, almost embarrassing, silence. Both sisters felt strange.

It was creepy.

Slowly Heather turned around and looked up at her younger sister. Phyllis saw that her eyelashes and cheeks were glinting-wet.

"To tell you the truth, Phyllis," she replied gently, "Mummy is worried about Thomas. You know that she has had seven of us so she should have some idea of what she is talking about. She thinks that Thomas' head should be a lot firmer by now than what it is."

Turning back down again at the children, Heather hastily brushed the tears from her cheeks with the side of her hand.

So that was it! Her worst fears had been realised. There WAS a difference between the two babies.

Both sisters wept unashamedly.

Now that it was all out in the open, they could talk about it. They could act on it too. Changing infants back and forward between them they compared their firmness. This exercise progressed to a comparison of every possible feature they could think of.

Now that she had confided her blackest fears to her own sister, Phyllis became more emotionally distressed.

Heather kept trying to console her. She assured her younger sister that if there was a difference, there would probably be some perfectly simple medical explanation for it.

"Just you stay here with me," Heather suggested, "My doctor will be calling this afternoon to see Carolyn. We will ask him what he thinks."

The next car to pull up at the house, however, was not the family G.P. It was Ethel Blakely! The young mothers' mother.

"What on earth is wrong with the pair of you?" she asked, as soon as she entered the living room. It didn't take her many seconds to size up the situation. Red eyes, and soggy hankies in clenched fists, were the sure giveaways.

"What's the truth of all this, Mummy?" Phyllis addressed her bewildered mother. "Do you think there is something the matter with Thomas?"

Mrs. Blakely stood still. She looked from Heather to Phyllis. Then from Thomas to Carolyn. She needed thinking time.

How was she going to tell her daughter what she really thought?

"Yes, Phyllis," she began lovingly. "I think his wee head should be firmer by now."

She paused for breath, but noticing the just-about-to-cry-again look come over the young mother's face, she went on hastily. "But don't panic. I would advise you to take him to the doctor and ask him to examine Thomas thoroughly."

"Well, actually, I have just told Phyllis to wait until my doctor calls this afternoon. I will ask him if he would have a look at Thomas," Heather informed her mother.

Mrs. Blakely was glad to hear that.

"Good idea," she said. "I will just stay too and hear what his opinion is."

And she did.

When the family doctor called, about an hour later, Heather met him in the kitchen. There was a whispered conversation.

As they approached the living room door, Phyllis could hear, through the chink that it had been left open, Heather preparing the doctor for what he might find.

"She is in here. She is really upset."

The doctor came into the living room, to Phyllis, who was cradling her treasured Thomas protectively in her arms.

Speaking quietly, he instructed Phyllis to lay him down on the floor. Then, getting down beside the baby, the doctor tried to lift him up.

As she watched the doctor examine Thomas, Phyllis was conscious of little things which she had noticed before, but hadn't dared to mention.

They didn't seem like little things now!

His head was floppy. Thomas could make no effort either to raise it up, or hold it up.

After completing an examination of the tiny arms and legs as well, the doctor agreed that, yes, he should probably be firmer by now.

Realising the emotional state that Phyllis was in, but also the medical implications of the situation, the doctor spoke kindly to the anxious mother.

"I would advise you to go, with Hertford, and take Thomas to see your own doctor as soon as possible," he counselled.

Phyllis had to wait until after the doctor had checked up on Carolyn, and then left.

Beyond that she couldn't stay.

"I must go home and find Hertford," she said, through her tears, to Heather and her mother.

Finding Hertford didn't prove too difficult. When the work in the fields was finished for the day, he started to clear out a sheugh on the lane. That way he could occupy his restless hands and brain, and he would also be in a position to greet his wife and son when they arrived home in time for tea.

He was pleased to recognise the engine noise. That was them coming now.'

When Phyllis pulled up beside him she wound down the window.

It didn't take more than one glance at her to establish that all was not well.

"What's wrong with you?" he asked.

"There's nothing wrong with me, but I think there is something wrong with Thomas," came the shock reply.

"What do you mean?" Hertford went on earnestly. He was stunned.

"Let's both go down to the house and we can talk it over," Phyllis proposed, in a voice that trembled with emotion.

Work was finished for good now.

Shouldering the shovel and the fork, Hertford followed the car, which had set off in a flurry of stones and dust, to the house.

When the car drove into the yard, Hertford's mother came over to it.

As Phyllis opened the door to get out, her mother-in-law asked, out of friendly interest, "Well, have you had a good day?"

Phyllis dissolved into tears. Again.

With that sickening sense of having unwittingly said the wrong thing, she asked considerately, "Is there something the matter with you, Phyllis?"

Opening another door of the car to lift Thomas out, the distraught young mother pointed to him and said, through her sobs, "Not with me. But with him."

Jean Arnold's face turned ashen pale.

The two women carried Thomas into the kitchen, and they were soon followed by Hertford.

When she had spread the changing mat on the large table in the kitchen, Phyllis laid Thomas down on it. Then she copied what the doctor had done. She raised him gently.

"Look at his head," she kept repeating. "Look at his head."

When her awestruck husband and his numbed mother did as she asked, they knew what she meant.

Thomas couldn't hold his head up. It just wobbled about. Or hung down limply.

Mrs. Arnold knew that they had to do something. They just couldn't stand there all afternoon, becoming more dejected.

"Hertford, you go and get changed," she ordered calmly.

"Then the pair of you take Thomas down to the doctor's right away."

They did just that.

In twenty minutes, all three of them were in the doctor's waiting room.

Although they only had to wait for ten minutes, it seemed like an eternity to Phyllis. She felt that all the others there were gazing at her.

They weren't, but she thought they were.

She felt that everybody knew that her baby "wasn't right."

They didn't, but she thought they did.

If they all knew, why, oh why, hadn't somebody told her? Why had she not caught it on herself by now?

It was a horrible sensation.

When the family doctor examined Thomas he was aware that Phyllis was jumping to all kinds of conclusions, possibly with some justification.

To clarify a potentially very worrying situation for everyone he made an appointment at the Lagan Valley Hospital, in Lisburn. Here Thomas would be seen by the gynaecologist who had attended his birth, and a paediatrician.

Hertford and Phyllis returned home, still perplexed, but with the minor consolation that somebody else was going to advise them about their little Thomas.

When the young parents attended that appointment in the Lagan Valley Hospital, about two weeks later, the gynaecologist spoke to them first.

"I will always remember the day that Thomas was born," he remarked. "There was great excitement in here."

Phyllis tried to smile.

"Yes, I remember that day well too! We are worried that there is something wrong with Thomas though," she replied.

Neither she nor her husband could have been prepared for the doctor's response.

"Well, we suspected that there was something the matter with Thomas, but we couldn't be absolutely sure. There was so much joy in both of your hearts that we thought it best to allow you to take him home. We knew that if there was a problem with him then it would become more evident and you would realise it yourselves with the passing of time," he said.

Hertford and Phyllis were dumbfounded. They just sat and stared at each other and then at baby Thomas, totally speechless.

"There is a paediatrician here, an expert in children's ailments," the doctor went on softly, "Don't be worrying yourself unduly. Your Thomas is a lovely wee boy. Everything possible will be done for him."

The examination of Thomas by the paediatrician was the most thorough to date. He tried to lift Thomas up, and observed his head movements. He worked with his arms and legs, tested his hands an d feet.

Throughout the examination Phyllis kept interrupting, asking questions. She was so uptight that she wanted to know what the expert thought - and sooner rather than later.

"What do you think?" she would ask.

"Can this be treated?" she would enquire.

Whilst the examinations were being carried out, however, she got no answers.

The paediatrician was intent on his work. He had to be sure of his diagnosis before he spoke.

When he did comment it was merely to tell Hertford and Phyllis that he would like Thomas to be seen by a specialist in the Royal Victoria Hospital.

He would arrange the appointment.

Thus the waiting, the worrying, the uncertainty, dragged on.

The specialist paediatrician in the Royal Victoria Hsoptial, Belfast, had Thomas admitted so that extensive tests could be carried out.

It was early June, and hot sunny weather. It was great weather for farmers but Hertford barely noticed it. Indeed

Spring had merged into Summer but for Hertford and Phyllis one long anxious day had just blurred into the next.

The type of weather, or the time of day, or night, had become an irrelevance to them.

Thomas, and his condition, had become an obsession.

On a Friday, in the middle of the month when the results of all the tests were collated, Hertford and Phyllis met with the specialist to hear the outcome. The final diagnosis.

"The scan has shown that a tiny part of the cerebellum is missing from Thomas' brain," the specialist explained. This was medical, technical.

Then came the hard part, the knock-out blow.

"As a result of this Thomas will neither be able to walk or talk or sit up unaided. He will be both physically and mentally handicapped."

The young couple were devastated.

Their eyes were open, but they were seeing nothing.

Their legs had suddenly become weak and shaky. They were too numb to cry.

"We will want to monitor his development. We will arrange another appointment for six week's time."

The doctor had finished all that she had to say so she slipped silently from the room. It hadn't been easy for her either.

Hertford and Phyllis were left with their baby, their tangled thoughts and their heavy hearts.

They were both weeping now.

When they regained sufficient composure to allow them to return to the car, it was like an oven. The summer sun was blazing down.

Thomas was placed into the back seat in his carry-cot. Sitll Hertford and Phyllis hadn't spoken a word to each other.

They didn't know what to say. What could they say?

As the drive homeward began, Phyllis was besieged by a guilt complex.

"God is punishing you Phyllis," her thoughts accused - "He has given you this baby because you have gone and married an unsaved man. You have backslidden and let Him down. You know what the Bible says, 'Don't be unequally yoked with unbelievers' ..."

Only sobs stirred the stillness. Their shared but silent sorrow was finding an emotional escape.

Hertford drove along with his elbow resting on the edge of the open window. As soon as one cigarette was finished he lit up another. Smoke drifted into the car and out into the shimmering heat.

His thoughts were about the rotten luck of it all.

"Four months ago I had a son and heir," he mused, "Now what have I got? And worse still, what can I do about it? If I could turn every sod on the farm into gold I still couldn't change a single thing."

They both so loved their little Thomas who knew nothing of their distress. He was sleeping peacefully in the back seat.

The young parents both felt so sick. They felt in some way 'let down' by somebody or something. Neither of them was quiite sure by whom, or by what. It was going to be hard to talk about it, too. How could they tell everybody?

It was Phyllis who spoke first, when they were almost home. Her opening remark was a kick-back against God.

"Why? Why? Why?" she agonised. "How could there be a God who could let something like this happen?"

Hertford had no time whatsoever for God.

"What are you talking about GOD for?" he retored fiercely, more from frustration than anger. "What has HE got to do with anything?"

CHAPTER FIVE

Coming To Terms

⚜ ⚜ ⚜

When they arrived home on that Friday evening Hertford and Phyllis each contacted their parents who had been waiting anxiously for news.

On hearing the final result as described by the Hospital paediatrician, and sensing how upset their children were, Tom and Ethel Blakely and Ford and Jean Arnold came down to the house immediately. They wanted to hear everything, every single word, that the doctors had said. They didn't want to miss a thing.

Hertford and Phyllis found a sense of relief in pouring out their hearts to their sympathetic parents. It was great to release their pent-up emotions into understanding ears.

Everyone was so sad. So sorry.

The muted conversations lasted late on into the evening and then on into the night.

Nobody wanted to go home.

Nobody wanted to go to bed.

Everybody felt that they should say something but nobody was quite sure of what to say. Conversations consisted of clipped sentences interspersed by sighs and tears.

Many cups of tea were poured, only to remain half-drunk and cold. Nibbled biscuits lay around.

There was a strange eerie feeling about the house. It was as though something had just started to die. It was like finding the first petals of a treasured rose bloom lying rain-spattered in the mud.

In the weeks that followed Hertford and Phyllis went through the trauma of explaining to family and friends the situation about Thomas.

They seemed to relive that hot June afternoon in the Royal at least once every day.

It came to the stage that it was like a drama which they had performed so often that they knew it perfectly. Both of them had their own particular lines off by heart.

The acquired ability to recount the story in its most minute detail didn't bring any consolation, however. Each explanation was an emotional trial.

It was the care and sympathy of friends and family which meant so much to the young parents. They all loved Thomas. They doted on him.

As the sense that they were being borne along by the genuine, heartfelt concern of others enveloped Phyllis and Hertford, they gradually, slowly, came to terms with the word "handicapped."

It had not been easy. It had been like recovering from a long and debilitating illness.

Things steadily began to return to normal. Normality meant something different now, though.

Hertford was back in t he yard and on the tractor. He felt himself compelled to make little excursions back to the house every now and again, however. Just to check that they were both O.K. Perhaps he expected there to be a dramatic and sudden improvement in Thomas's condition. A miracle perhaps?

It didn't occur.

For Phyllis, normality meant adapting to a new routine, an entirely different lifestyle.

Her little Thomas had to be taken each week to Craigavon Hospital to be exercised. These weekly visits to Hospital proved to be a double benefit for her.

Firstly, she realised that she didn't have the only physically and mentally handicapped baby in the North of Ireland. There were others, just like Thomas. Other parents were coping with the same dilemma. This was comforting.

The second way in which these hospital appointments helped her was that she came in contact with well-informed and caring nursing staff. They always had time for her. She was able to pour out her heart to them. To tell them of all her worries and concerns, however minor.

She was always given a kind and considerate response to all her queries. This made her feel better. Indeed she began to get the impression that she was in some way privileged to have a child like Thomas, so that shed learnt all these things.

Putting on a brave face in public was what Hertford and Phyllis found most difficult to get used to. Taking Thomas to visit friends, especially those who had normal children, was tough at first.

They faced up to it with a smile on a quivering lip. With an eye where the sparkle of pride was misted by a tear.

People were really understanding. It was never so painful, second time around.

Thus when the young parents began to recognise that Thomas was accepted, just for who he was, by family and friends, they felt more content.

It inspired a degree of confidence in the flagging, flattened soul.

Phyllis and Hertford had to be happy for Thomas.

They couldn't be anything else, after the initial shock, and then the gradual coming to terms, for he in himself was such a happy child.

In his own little world, Thomas was oblivious to the anxieties of the world of adults. He just chuckled and bubbled his way through every day, unaware of the concern of his loving parents and interested family circle.

When they had become reconciled to the fact that Thomas would always be unable to do the things that most other children did, but that he was special, very special, in his own particular way, a question cropped up in the minds of his parents.

They were both worried about it as individuals.

Then they shared it with each other.

The medical profession assured them that they shouldn't have any need to worry about it.

That didn't stop them from being apprehensive, all the same.

Often, as they lifted their baby, or fed him, or drove him to or from his exercise sessions, it drifted, like a bad dream, into, and around their minds. It threatened to destroy their shared vision of a big happy family around a big homely table.

It was simply this.

Could it happen again?

CHAPTER SIX

Ford

✤ ✤ ✤

The deepest misgivings of Hertford and Phyllis were soon to be put to the test. In late summer 1984 Phyllis found out that she was expecting a second baby.

Now the anxiety really began in earnest.

Despite telling themselves that it probably wouldn't happen again. "Not so soon, surely."

Still they worried.

Despite even more medical assurances that the chances of their having another handicapped baby were 'one in a million'.

Still they worried.

Having learnt to cope with all of Thomas's special needs they loved him dearly.

Inwardly, secretly, however, they longed for another child who would fulfil a dual role.

Their hope was that the new addition to their family would be good company for Thomas. That would be very important.

Secondly, they would just appreciate it so much if he or she could be like what everybody else's babies seemed to be. Physically and mentally normal.

No exercise sessions. No special diets. No particular demands of any kind.

Just normal.

As the year progressed, so did Thomas. He was growing steadily and had started to feed better, provided that everything was well mashed down. He couldn't manage big bites or large lumps.

He was now accepted by everybody. All his relatives had 'a soft spot' for him, probably because of his disability. His young parents were becoming daily more confident in dealing with his requirements.

When Christmas 1984 came, Phyllis remembered her prediction of the previous year.

Yes. There were three of them now.

She had been right about that.

Yes. They did have a baby to share everything with.

She had been right about that as well.

But there were ways in which the reality of Christmas 1984 differed from the mental picture which she had painted for herself at Christmas 1983.

Thomas was eleven months old. But he couldn't sit up, or crawl. He couldn't even hold his head up ...

In seasons of silent reflection such thoughts would sneak stealthily into her mind.

She couldn't entertain them though. Wiping away an infrequent, but nonetheless real, lonely tear, she would think positively. She had to.

And what joy it brought.

Christmas 1984 was a happy time for all three of them. Hertford and Phyllis made sure of that. Thomas meant so much to them. They would do everything to ensure that he was comfortable and content.

Then there was this other baby to come. What would he or she be like?

Contemplating the birth of their second child brought mixed feelings. It was a restrained pleasure. Like being forced to stifle a hearty sneeze. They were both excited and scared all at once.

Time, as it so often does, brought the answer to their uncertainty. An end to all the edgy speculation.

On 29th April, 1985, their second baby, another boy, was born in Craigavon Hospital

A few minute after his birth, a doctor came out of the theatre and assured Hertford that this recent addition to their family was completely normal.

"He is a great little boy. He is as strong as a bull," were his words.

About ten minutes later a nurse brought the infant out for Hertford to see. When he saw the little bundle of humanity pulling up his legs and waving his arms about, he realised what the doctor had said had been true. He was witnessing it now with his own wondering eyes.

What a relief to the anxious father. All the worry of the past nine months seemed to evaporate in a split second. He was walking on air!

When Phyllis came round from sedation and was told that her baby was normal, she could hardly believe it. It was brilliant.

Could it really be true?

Like her husband before her, she needed convincing.

Proof was at hand. By a hand.

The gynaecologist came into the ward, and placing the new baby on the bed beside his proud mother, he slipped his finger into the infant's hand.

Instantly the tiny hand grasped the finger. And held on.

Such a simple thing! Yet for Phyllis how sweet! It conveyed such a tremendous message!

Yes! It was true. This child was normal. Ordinary. Just like all the others all around.

It was great!

Their fears had been groundless. It hadn't happened again.

When Hertford returned to his wife's bedside, to speak to Phyllis, and gaze in admiration at his infant son, they decided that he should be called Ford. This had been predetermined for months. It just required the rubber stamp of mutual approval, now that their baby had arrived safely.

A few hours later, Hertford decided that he should probably go home. As he rose to go he said to Phyllis, "I will tell my Da that this one's normal, and called after him."

He had crossed the ward, but before he could finally drag himself away he turned back and looked at little Ford.

"I wonder will this fella be able to work on the farm?" he mused.

Hertford was seeing one of his aspirations realised. A son and heir of the kind he had always imagined.

CHAPTER SEVEN

'Heaven's Very Special Child'

✤ ✤ ✤

After Hertford had gone, Phyllis sat on the edge of her bed, taking a leisurely look around her little private ward, savouring her surroundings.

Sleeping in the cot beside her was baby Ford. On top of the locker were a pair of ornamental blue boots with yellow crocuses growing in them. Hertford had been out to do some shopping, after he had seen his newborn son!

As the news of this second child for Hertford and Phyllis began to filter through the Arnold and Blakely network, the bouquets began to arrive.

Flowers seemed to grace every useable space.

When the door was knocked, Phyllis called "Come in!" cheerily, expecting to see another orderly arrive into the ward with yet another bunch of carnations or chrysanthemums.

She was mildly surprised, then, to see the door edged open very gingerly, tentatively.

A nurse who Phyllis didn't recognise slipped softly into the ward.

"Hello, Mrs. Arnold," the visitor began. "You probably don't know me, but I know you. May I come in a minute?"

"Certainly! Come on in!" Phyllis welcomed the opportunity to speak to someone. She felt in the mood for a chat and usually found it more satisfying to talk to a person than a bunch of daffodils.

"I have seen you coming and going to physiotherapy with Thomas over this last year," the caller explained. "I am just up here to congratulate you on having another wee boy. It is great to hear that everything is O.K. too. I'm delighted for you."

Phyllis warmed to this kind nurse right away. And the kind nurse knew what to do next.

Leaning over the cot, she admired baby Ford.

After she had gone through the whole range of the "weight-at-birth" type questions, she plunged straight into the "who-do-you-think-he-is-like?" routine.

Typical mother stuff.

In the course of conversation Phyllis learnt that her newly-found friend had two children, one of whom was handicapped. The other was a normal, healthy, active child.

That 'rang a bell' with Phyllis. Wasn't that her family situation now as well?

As she rose to go the nurse said quietly, "Phyllis, I have a poem here that has been a great help to me. I would like you to read it sometime at your leisure. Perhaps it will help you to understand about Thomas. Understand, I mean, that he is a very special child. And indeed you could find that you and your husband are very privileged people too. God has chosen you both for a specific purpose. To care for His very special child. I think this poem will make that plain."

Phyllis was interested.

"What's the poem called?" she enquired.

"It is called, 'Heaven's Very Special Child,'" the nurse replied, as she offered the young mother a sheet of folded paper.

"Thanks very much, I will read it right now," was the eager response.

As Phyllis unfolded the paper, her visitor walked slowly towards the door.

"I have stayed long enough," she remarked. "I will go and leave you in peace, Phyllis."

With that she disappeared, just as silently and gracefully as she had come.

Phyllis swung her legs up onto the bed, then propped herself up on the pillows.

Whatever this poem was about, it must be very important. A nurse had considered it worthwhile to seek her out, and come up to her little private ward to give it to her. She was determined, therefore, that she was going to enjoy it.

When she had made herself comfortable, opened out then flattened out, the piece of paper which she had been given, this is what she read:-

"Heaven's Special Child"

A meeting was held quite far from the earth,
"It's time again for another birth."
Said the angels to the Lord above,
"This Special Child will need much love.

His progress may seem very slow.
Accomplishments he may not show.
And he'll require much extra care,
From the folks he meets down there.

He may not run, or laugh or play,
His thoughts may seem quite far away.
In many ways he won't adapt,
And he'll be known as 'handicapped'.

So let's be careful where he's sent,
We want his life to be content.
Please Lord find the parents who,
Will do this special job for You.

They will not realise right away,
This lending role they're asked to play.
But with this child sent from above,
Comes stronger faith and richer love.

And soon they'll know the privilege given,
In caring for this child from Heaven.
Their precious child so meek and mild,
Is Heaven's Very Special Child."

Having read the poem through once, Phyllis felt compelled to read it again. Then again. And again.

It gripped her. It transfixed her.

After the fourth or fifth reading there came over her a strange sensation. It was as though time had put on its brakes.

She experienced a sense of being suspended between heaven and earth.

It was a sense of God.

April sunlight streamed in through the window. The clusters of flowers stood about like guardians of the heavenly realms. Colourful celestial custodians.

Little Ford snuffled and wriggled occasionally.

Many of the lines that she had read struck home to her heart.

"He may not run, or laugh, or play!"

It had been some experience coming to terms with that realisation.

"And he'll be known as 'handicapped'".

There was that word again!

Hertford and she had spent many agonising months learning to entertain that word in their thoughts not to mention speaking it from their lips.

It seemed so harsh. So real. So cold. When you saw it in print.

"Handicapped!"

But then the underlying message of the poem was new. Different. A new light in an old gloom.

"Please Lord find the parents who,
Will do this special job for You."
Were she and Hertford really THAT 'special'?
Could they be, actually, 'special' to God?
Well, yes. They had been giving little Thomas "the much extra care" that he required.
Rung number one on God's ladder of 'Special' was mounted.
They had been able to adapt to the recognition that "in many ways" Thomas wouldn't 'adapt'. It had taken them some time, but they got there. Eventually.
Now they were two steps up. And climbing.
Had they not developed a much richer bond of love as a result of their shared experiences in that first year with Thomas?
Of course they had.
Phyllis was beginning to feel good about all this. Congratulate herself. Feel smug, almost.
There were three ways at least in which they were special to God.
Three rungs up the ladder. And climbing.
Then came the shock.
When Phyllis reached forward to put her foot on the next step of this imaginary ladder to God which she was mounting with growing enthusiasm, it wasn't there!
There was a rung missing!
There was a great gaping hole where the next step should have been!
She was on the ladder of Special.
She was up the ladder of Special.
She was STUCK on the ladder of Special.
What about the "stronger faith"?
The challenge plunged like an arrow into the heart of the young mother.
"Stronger faith."
Where WAS her faith in God?
Buried. Hidden. Forgotten.

God spoke directly to Phyllis through an awakened conscience in the sunlit solitude of that private ward.

In His Divine wisdom, God had arranged for her to be left undisturbed for twenty minutes, alone with her thoughts.

The bouquet-bearers had stopped knocking and her baby son was asleep. His tiny mouth opened in a tiny yawn every so often.

All was still.

Phyllis, allowed the poem sheet to rest on the bedclothes before her.

She felt happy and sad, mixed up and guilty, all at once.

As she scrutinised every inch of the tiny body of her infant son, again and again, as he lay there beside her, pefectly healthy and blissfully asleep, she felt grateful to God and ashamed of hersself.

She had been wrong to be so harsh. It had been one big mistake to presume that God had been punishing her.

"Heaven's Very Special Child" put a whole new complexion on the situation. It was somthing she had never even thought about before.

Lying right back on the pillows, Phyllis closed her eyes. As she did so, a welling-up tear overflowed down her cheek.

"Lord, please forgive me," she prayed, silently, earnestly.

"Forgive me for thinkiing that You were punishing me by giving me Thomas. I see now the reason for it all."

Pausing a moment, she opened her eyes to check on little Ford, then closed them again to continue fervently.

"Lord, I want to come back to You. Help me. Help me, please. I'm so sorry. I have so much to thank You for. Thank You for Hertford. Thank You for Thomas. And thank You for this lovely, normal baby boy."

Her prayer ended with a heartfelt request for Divine assitance. She had been away too long from God.

It had been a struggle, trying to cope, without His power.

"Help me to be strong, Lord," she begged.

"I want to be strong for Hertford."

"I need to be strong for Thomas."

"I would like to be strong for Ford."

"And I would love to be strong for You."

When she reopened her eyes, the Spring sunlight still streamed into the ward.

The flowers still held their heads up high.

Ford was still sound asleep.

Phyllis was aware of a glowing radiance on her cheek.

She was also aware of a growing peace within her heart.

She had started out on the long road back.

CHAPTER EIGHT

Moving House

✤ ✤ ✤

When Phyllis came home from Hospital, she was now a mother of two. She had two equally loved, but very different, sons.

Summer was approaching and the young parents looked forward to long sunny days with the windows and doors of their little house wide open, and their two infant boys lying outside in the garden.

It didn't work out that way.

The summer of 1985 turned out to be one of the wettest for many years. It seemed to rain every single day.

Their house began to show signs of damp. Phyllis became uneasy. She couldn't ever seem to get it dried out.

One thing that didn't worry her though, was the feeding of Ford in the night.

A few minutes at the Aga heated the bottle, Ford downed it in ten minutes, and everyone was back to sleep again! Great!

The wet summer progressed into a wet autumn.

The barley crop was lost. Flattened by rain and soaking wet, it couldn't be saved.

Ford senior, Hertford's father, bought some sheep to put into it. They could either eat it up or tramp it down, leaving the fields ready for ploughing again.

It was a major problem for Ford the father and Hertford the son. Ford the grandson wasn't too bothered about barley.

Not yet, anyway.

The continuing wet weather brought with it continued and somewhat worsened dampness in the young couple's home.

Phyllis was concerned about Thomas. He seemed to develop colds very easily. At times she worried about his health. She was convinced that the damp conditions in which they were living were contributing, at least in some way, to Thomas's frequent colds.

One day, when Mrs. Arnold called to see Phyllis and the boys, and help where necessary, Phyllis voiced her anxiety to her mother-in-law.

"I'm a bit worried about Thomas," she began.

"What do you mean, 'worried about him'? In what way?"

Jean Arnold was only mildly concerned. She was sitting looking at Thomas and he seemed to be perfectly O.K.

"It's nothing serious," Phyllis reassured her. "It's just that with this house being so damp and the winter coming on, I'm afraid that these colds which Thomas keeps catching will get worse. All this damp just can't be good for him. You know what I mean?"

Jean did understand her daughter-in-law's deep disquiet. And she was so practical. If there was a sensible solution to an everyday problem, Jean would find it.

"Well, I tell you what to do," she suggested. "Why don't the four of you move up with us for the winter at least. We have spare bedrooms now as you know."

That was the answer!

Phyllis didn't need a lot of persuasion!

Thus it was that, in October 1985, Hertford, Phyllis, Thomas and Ford moved in to share the Arnold family home.

Initially, their intention was to winter there.

There was no big flit. Hertford and Phyllis just carried the most urgently needed of their bits and pieces across the yard, as and when they were required.

It proved to be a prudent move.

The young parents now had a large en-suite bedroom. Everywhere was carpeted.

No terrazza tiles in the middle of the night here! No standing with one foot in the oven!

Thomas and Ford had their own bedroom. It was ideal for them. A big bedroom with dry walls.

Their caring parents repapered it for them, and the paper actually stuck to the walls! They did it with nursery paper - all kittens and balloons, rainbows and clouds.

There was a white carpet on the floor.

Hertford and Phyllis wanted it to be ever so cosy for their two little sons.

And it was.

Moving up to the "big house" reminded Phyllis of her Blakely days. She liked going upstairs to bed!

They had space to spread themselves now, in this larger house.

A family friend made a special play pen for Thomas. Since he was a big child for his age, but unable to stand up, his play pen had to be more spacious than normal. This almost two metres square play pen sat in the middle of the floor in a large downstairs room.

Thomas lay in it quite contentedly, rolling over every so often.

For Hertford and Phyllis, life settled into another new, but soon to become normal, routine.

Phyllis still had to take Thomas for his hospital appointments. Then there were his exercise sessions, and longer feeding periods.

Since she was compelled to spend so much time on Thomas and his ongoing needs, Phyllis had less time than she would have liked to devote to her younger son, Ford.

That is where her mother-in-law proved to be such a tremendous help. She played the role of mother to Ford. Whilst Phyllis was attending to Thomas, whether nursing, feeding or changing, "Granny Jean", as she became affectionately known, was doing the same for Ford.

As Christmas approached, Hertford and Phyllis had to do some shopping. They had more enthusiasm for it this year. They felt that they were privileged to have two sons, with their different needs, to cater for.

For Thomas they bought the usual array of rattles and cuddly, squeaky and musical toys. Much the same as the previous year, really.

But for Ford they had different ideas.

He was going to be a farmer, wasn't he?

Just like Granda Ford and his daddy.

So they bought him a tractor. A big blue one with a red trailer. Had to give him the right ideas! Start him off on the right wheels!

Not as part of his Christmas presents, but as something they were convinced he needed, they bought Ford a walkie-pen.

When they put him into it at first he just hung there, gazing around. Then he discovered that if he moved his feet this thing moved as well.

In just a few days he was zooming around the downstairs of the house.

As Thomas lay in his play pen, listening to his musical toys, his younger brother was going around the play pen, making his own way about. He discovered that the family table was high enough to allow him to duck down, get underneath it, and come out on the other side.

How he loved that!

Christmas Eve, 1985, was so exciting for Hertford and Phyllis. Now they had two children to share it with. And Hertford's parents, their kind and patient hosts.

Phyllis so enjoyed wrapping up the presents that Christmas Eve. It reminded her, too, of childhood days in the Blakely home, when she used to 'hang up her stocking'.

Same excitement. Same sense of anticipation.

Only now the satisfaction would be in observing the pleasure of Thomas with his presents, and the excitement of Ford in receiving his.

She wasn't disappointed.

For her, and her husband, and for them all as a family, that Christmas was really something.

The deep warmth of togetherness felt that Day was evident in a simple situation which arose.

The sturdy box in which the big blue tractor had come lay abandoned in the middle of the living room floor. Some roughly-torn Christmas paper still clung valiantly to its side. It was surrounded by all the Christmas fripperies that make the festive season so special. Bows, tags, coloured ribbons.

Someone lifted Thomas and set him into the large box, taking care to prop him up in the corner. Noticing that there was still some space left in the corner diagonally opposite, someone else lifted Ford and placed him in it.

Phyllis rushed for the camera. She wanted to record the moment. As she put the viewfinder up to her eye, she felt complete, somehow.

There was a sense in which she had in some way "arrived".

At least one of their dreams had come true.

Thomas had company. And it was tailor-made for him!

It was his own little brother!

CHAPTER NiNE

First Steps

✤ ✤ ✤

With Christmas over, the New Year had begun. And what a start!

Phyllis found out that she was expecting a third baby.

She and Hertford weren't concerned about this at all, however. In fact, they were extremely pleased.

Thomas was progressing, slowly but surely, within the limits of what he would ever be able to achieve, and Ford was growing normally. It was an absorbing exercise for the young parents, to compare his development with that of Thomas, at the various ages and stages.

A third child would fill another chair around the big table, eventually, no doubt. Their family dream was being realised, as fast, if not faster, than they had anticipated. The terrific thing about having a third member in their family was that he or she would be an able and active playmate for Ford.

Wasn't the probability of their having another handicapped child just 'one in a million'?

It would be great to have them all so close together too, they reckoned. This meant that they would all grow up together and be company for one another.

Marvellous.

In late May, 1986, they embarked upon something which Hertford and Phyllis had often dreamed of. Something they used to talk about by the fireside on long, dark, stormy winter evenings.

It was a family holiday. Just the four of them together. Having time to spend with Thomas and Ford.

In order to allow them to cater for their children's specific individual needs, Hertford and Phyllis went to stay in Phyllis's father's caravan in Castlerock for a week.

How they looked forward to it!

Talked about it! Planned it!

When the big day came, and they arrived at the caravan which was to double as their family home for the next week, it was raining. Not untypical for Northern Ireland, but likewise not ideal for the start of a caravan holiday.

Sitting in the car they decided upon their plan of action.

"You stay in the car with the boys, Hertford," Phyllis suggested to her husband. "I'll get into the 'van and check that everything is O.K. Then you can bring the children in."

That agreed, Phyllis dashed over to the caravan, opened up, and stepped inside. She was met by that furniture-and-fabric-flavoured frowstiness which is a characteristic of closed-up caravans.

After opening a few windows, "to let in a breath of fresh air," she made a quick inspection to satisfy herself that all was in order. Then she went to the caravan door and signalled to Hertford to bring in the children.

As Ford would be easier to transport, his dad decided to take him in first. Having carried his younger son over to the caravan door, he reached in as far as he could, and placed him on the floor. Then he turned away, to turn his attention to Thomas.

It was then that the unexpected occurred.

Phyllis had been trying to figure out the complexities of getting the table up. She glanced over to check that Ford was safe.

Then she just stared. He had pushed himself up on to his feet. There he stood, swaying gently.

Suddenly, deliberately, he walked towards his mother.

Phyllis was awestruck.

By the time Hertford returned to the caravan door with Thomas, Phyllis was hugging Ford warmly

"Do you know what has just happened there, Hertford?" she began, not knowing whether to laugh or cry. Her husband didn't know what had happened, and he was totally at a loss to know what to make of the look of pleasant consternation on his wife's face.

"Ford has just walked over to me," she exclaimed, almost triumphantly.

When Thomas had been laid on a couch, Hertford had to witness this latest stage in his son's development for himself.

Completely ignoring the fact that the luggage was still out in the car, and the car door was lying open in the rain, Hertford placed Ford at the opposite end of the caravan.

Holding out his arms, he made the simple request, "Come to daddy."

Little Ford did just that.

He pushed himself up to a standing position, paused a moment to establish his balance, then came to daddy! On his own two feet!

What joy! What excitement!

Ford looked no end of pleased with himself. He wasn't a baby any more. He was a toddler now!

Phyllis and Hertford were thrilled.

This was their second son, but the first to walk.

The remainder of that holiday was spent encouraging Ford to develop confidence in his newly-acquired skill.

The change in content of the please-walk-for-us-Ford stimuli emphasised their closeness as a family unit.

Simple commands to 'come to mummy' or 'come to daddy' developed naturally into useful requests like, "Bring over that rattle for Thomas," or "Take that biscuit to Thomas."

Whilst they were delighted at the sense of family cooperation that Ford's learning to walk had brought, it also highlighted something else for Hertford and Phyllis.

They were inclined to be sorry, but had to be sensible about it.

It was an inescapable fact.

The gap between the natural capabilities of their two little sons was widening.

CHAPTER TEN

Not Again Lord!?

✠ ✠ ✠

In late September 1986, Phyllis was in hospital again, awaiting the birth of their third child.

"Will it be a girl this time?" she wondered idly, now and
again. She wasn't really fussed about the gender of her next
baby, as long as he or she would be healthy and well.

Lying there in the ward she committed herself to the Lord
once more.

"Please, Lord, let everything be all right," she prayed.

Phyllis felt confident that her prayer would be answered.
So confident indeed, that it was almost one of those I-know-
that-it-will-be-O.K.-but-I-thought-I-had-better-mention-it-to-
You-anyway-Lord kind of prayers.

Thomas was one in a million. So he was going to be the
only one of his kind in the family. In the big happy family ...

As she drifted back into consciousness after the birth Phyllis
heard a nurse's voice. It seemed to echo from far away.

"Wake up now, Mrs. Arnold," the distant voice was saying.
"You have another little boy. He has lovely red hair. His daddy
will be all pleased."

Phyllis heard.

What she heard, though, was not what they said. It was
what they didn't say.

There was no, "Normal. Healthy. Fine. O.K. All right."

A sense of apprehension gripped her. It was an intuitive premonition.

A baffling sense of blackness enveloped her soul.

All was not well. She knew it.

She couldn't explain it.

She just knew it.

As her mind became clearer, she began to ask questions of the nurses who were busily working away around her.

They answered her as best they could.

Direct questions received indirect answers.

"Where's Hertford? When can I see my husband?" Phyllis enquired of them.

"He will be in to see you in a few minutes, Mrs. Arnold. Don't worry yourself now."

The nurses tried to reassure her, but to no avail.

There was something wrong with the baby.

Phyllis was convinced of that.

Some strange maternal instinct had been aroused in her - and she was so sure it was right.

Who would be the first to tell her the truth? To come out with it straight?

Meanwhile, Hertford was waiting outside the theatre. Impatiently. Pacing up and down.

He was aware of an unusual coming and going, 'to-ing and fro-ing', in and out of the theatre. A specialist whom Hertford recognised had gone in.

When a nurse emerged with a tiny bundle wrapped in a blanket, Hertford stepped forward to see what it was.

"You have another little son, Mr. Arnold," she said, forcing a smile which should have come easily. She appeared somewhat concerned.

Hertford caught a glimpse of the top of a baby's head, with its 'lovely red hair'. It was just like his own in colour, but it was very much finer, and there certainly was a lot of it!

"Is he O.K.?" was the proud father's question.

His enquiry was greeted with an evasive answer, also.

"I am just taking him to have him checked over right now," the nurse replied, then hurried off up the corridor, carrying Hertford's third son out of sight.

A deep disquiet stirred within him.

"That's funny," he mused as he stood puzzled and motionless in the corridor. "When Ford was born they came out and told me he was normal. 'Strong as a bull' was what they said."

He was engrossed in persuading himself that it was 'only routine', when Phyllis was wheeled out of the theatre on her way back to the ward.

Hertford was invited to follow.

When Phyllis had been made comfortable in the ward, her husband chatted to her. They tried to talk about their new baby.

Both of them found it difficult.

A giant shadow hung over them, darkening their way ahead.

Any talk there was centred around his 'lovely red hair'.

Hertford knew from the nurse's comment, and countenance, that all was not well. He was trying manfully to hide his misgivings from Phyllis.

He didn't need to.

With that uncanny intuition, she was certain that there was something amiss as well.

Lying back on the pillows Phyllis just wept silently.

She was weak after the birth, befuddled by the anaesthetic and sick at heart.

About an hour later Tom and Ethel Blakely entered the ward. Phyllis saw them coming. Her mother was carrying a blue toy elephant and a bunch of flowers.

"I believe it is a wee red head," Tom began cheerily.

Phyllis exploded into loud uncontrollable sobs.

Mother placed the stuffed elephant and the bunch of flowers on the bed and put an arm around her daughter.

"What's wrong, Phyllis? What's wrong?" she enquired, her voice warm with love, urgent with anguish.

"It's the baby!" Phyllis blurted out. "I know, I just KNOW that there is something wrong with him."

Tom Blakely kicked the end of the bed in frustration.

"No, Phyllis! No!" he almost shouted. "Don't talk nonsense! It can't have happened again! Not again!"

Ethel showed her mother love.

"Don't worry about it, Phyllis," she comforted. "Hertford and your daddy will go and find out something from somebody."

Hertford had no real desire to find out any more than he already knew. He had, however an urgent desire to get out of that ward.

So he went.

His father-in-law followed, only to stop in the corridor.

When Hertford reached the Baby Unit, he was alone.

Seeing a lady doctor there whom he recognised, Hertford approached her. Not being a man of many words at the best of times, Hertford hadn't a lot to say now.

"Well, doctor?" he asked, making a profound enquiry with only two words.

It was enough for the doctor. She understood.

She shook her head.

"All is not right, I'm afraid," she replied.

Turning quickly away, Hertford left the Baby Unit. There was nothing left to say. He returned to the ward rather more slowly.

When he approached his wife's bedside, she was anxious for news.

"Well, what did they say?" Phyllis asked earnestly. "What is he like?"

One of these questions her husband could answer. The other one he couldn't. He just couldn't bring himself to tell the truth. The whole truth.

"Oh, he's lovely," Hertford began, with all the enthusiasm he could muster. "You want to see his lovely red hair. They are having a bit of a problem getting him to feed though, so they are not going to bring him up to you tonight."

"But is he all right? O.K.? Normal?" Phyllis persisted.

"He certainly looks all right," her husband replied.

That bit was true.

He did.

Making the excuse that Phyllis was exhausted and needed to rest, Hertford went home, heavy hearted.

On the next evening, visitors began to gather around the bed, but Phyllis wasn't content.

She wanted to see her third little son, Wendsley, as they agreed he should be called.

Hertford pushed Phyllis along the corridor to the Baby Unit, to satisfy that maternal craving to be with her child. All the visitors, who were mostly brothers and sisters of the new mum and dad, straggled along behind in a higgeldy-piggeldy procession.

The young parents entered the Baby Unit, leaving the other visitors to observe the proceedings through a viewing window.

It was going to be difficult to have their first together-viewing of their third baby in such public circumstances. Especially when what Phyllis suspected, Hertford already knew.

Phyllis sat in a chair, and a nurse handed her baby son into her arms.

When the tiny red head fell back limply over her arm, Phyllis experienced the same hollow sensation as she had done with Thomas.

She KNEW now, definitely, that this baby was handicapped, as well.

She just wept. Tears streamed down her face unchecked.

The visitors slipped silently away from the window, one by one.

A numbness came over Phyllis. It was that awful sense of living-death again.

When Hertford returned his by-now almost despondent wife to the ward, little was said.

This was yet another of those "what-do-you-say-in-a-fix-like-this?" situations.

Hertford went home, promising Phyllis that he would be back to see her, "first thing in the morning".

When he did return, as pledged, next morning, two doctors invited both Phyllis and he down to the Baby Unit.

The purpose of this consultation turned out to be mainly to formalise for the young parents what they already knew intuitively.

This was it. Officially.

"We thought you ought to know, Mr. and Mrs. Arnold," they explained, "that this baby appears to be like Thomas in every way in which we have been able to test him. This is totally contrary to all our expectations. But sadly, it is a fact."

The doctors then went on to assure the totally devastated couple of their support at all times. They also promised them, kindly, that Wendsley would receive the same high level of care that was being afforded to Thomas.

Hertford and Phyllis heard little of it.

They both had the same instant reaction.

It was simultaneous. It was sincere.

It was sad.

They both felt that they must get out of the Hospital. And sooner rather than later. They just wanted to be together, on their own, with their children and their thoughts.

Although what appeared to be emotionally imperative seemed medically inadvisable, the hospital staff agreed to allow Phyllis to go home with Hertford and baby Wendsley.

As they drove home that day they were both in mental torment once more.

Now they had three children under four years of age, and two of them were handicapped.

Phyllis was inclined to blame God for punishing her yet again.

"Heaven's Very Special Child" had been acceptable. Once.

She could have believed it. Once.

She had even felt good about it, in a peculiar sort of way. Once.

But surely even God couldn't expect them to take it a second time. Not twice.

Was it not rather unfair of God to expect them to rear two of these "very special" children? What about all the other parents around the countryside? Why not share the very special children out a bit? Let somebody else be "special" parents, just for a change?

Phyllis sat in the car, staring blankly ahead of her, in bitter silence of soul. She daren't voice her thoughts to her husband.

Hertford was as hard as a stone.

"God. Who is God? What has He got to do with anything?"

That had been his response nearly four years ago.

It would be even worse now.

CHAPTER ELEVEN

The Chicken House

✤ ✤ ✤

After the initial shock, the icy bitterness of heart melted away more quickly for Hertford and Phyllis with their third son, than it had done with the first. There were three reasons for this.

Firstly, they 'knew the ropes'. They knew how to cope with a disabled child. Having acquired all the skills and processes, and all the special adaptations of feeding and care required, with Thomas, coping with Wendsley was relatively easier.

Then there was the dreaded 'how-will-we-face-the-people?' fear. The 'what-do-we-say-to-them'? dilemma.

That was gone. Having been through it once and found the family circle most supportive, and the Great General Public to be sympathetic or at least, tolerant, Hertford and Phyllis had no problems in that regard either.

And thirdly, there were Hertford's parents. Coming back., as they did, from Hospital to the family home, meant that there were two more sets of eyes to watch the boys, two more pairs of hands to help.

Jean was marvellous.

Gradually, however, Hertford and Phyllis began to feel that seven of them were too many now, all living under one roof.

The three boys would be company for each other, it was true, but with two of them being handicapped, Phyllis knew that inevitably they would begin to clutter up the place with the special equipment required. For two of them. Special feeding chairs, play pens, exercise mats, all took up valuable space.

Added to that, there was Ford. At the age of eighteen months he had now become very independent. He could go to the fridge and get a drink for himself, or to go to a cupboard and help himself to a sweet - and to many another thing besides, as it took his fancy!

Phyllis was going to learn to appreciate Ford's ability to fetch and carry in the coming days, as his two brothers grew older.

The stairs posed another problem. Thomas was eating well at his special diet, and was thriving. This meant he was putting on weight. Getting heavier fast. But he was 'dead weight' to carry up and down the stairs.

It was true that Phyllis liked to go 'up the stairs to bed'. She didn't however, fancy having to transport two handicapped sons up and down the stairs for the rest of her days. Another consideration.

Then what about Jean and Ford, senior? Although they never once complained, in fact they rather appeared to enjoy the company, yet it was their house. Their home. Hertford and Phyllis had plonked themselves, plus three, by invitation, in it. Anyway, it wasn't fair, they reasoned, and it wouldn't be fair in the future, to ask Hertford's parents to live through the emotional, and indeed physical, problems of their daily routine.

One night, as they lay in bed, discussing the whole situation, the young couple came to the conclusion that the solution would be for them to build their own bungalow. It would have to be a bungalow for the boys. Stairs weren't on.

A bungalow of their own would be the answer.

But the dream answer posed a down-to-earth question. Money.

Which in their case they had not got. At least, not enough to build a bungalow with.

There was a practical answer to that question, they decided, at length.

They would build and run their own chicken house. That was, of course, provided Hertford's father would be agreeable. Ford Arnold already had four broiler chicken houses, which Hertford helped to manage.

If he only had one! Just one, of his own!

Then they could make enough, through time, to be self-sufficient.

That was the plan. They were enthusiastic about it.

A business. Then a bungalow.

That was the answer! No doubt about it!

Yet before they could see a brick built, or hear a chicken cheep, there were enquiries to be made, permission to be sought.

Hertford knew how to approach the subject.

Like many another young man in life, he considered that the best way to obtain anything from his parents was to find his mother on her own sometime, and 'in a good mood'. He would then tactfully raise the issue with her.

His mother was a good thermometer, he always felt. You could usually gauge the family temperature by a reading of her reactions.

Thus, late one evening, as he and his mother were sitting chatting by the Aga, Hertford seized his opportunity. Phyllis and the boys were all in bed, fast asleep, and his father was out in the yard.

"Hi, Ma, Phyllis and I would like to build our own bungalow," he began. "But I'm sure you have a fair idea that we haven't the money. We were thinking we could start our own chicken house to make a pound or two. Then if that worked out we could build our own bungalow."

Jean Arnold remained silent, but smiled encouragingly, as Hertford continued, "Do you think Da would agree to all that?

Do you think he would give us a site for a bungalow?"

When he had asked the second question, Hertford stopped. He stretched out in the armchair. He had finished. Said his piece. Done his bit.

Never mind Da for the minute, what was Ma going to say about it all?

He needn't have worried. Jean was happy enough.

She had felt for some time that for everybody's sake it would be best for the young family to make it on their own. This scheme that Hertford had just outlined so clearly would give them an independent income, with which they could eventually build a home of their own, in which to raise their family.

She liked the sound of it. And said so.

"I think he probably would," Jean replied. "I will speak to him about it later."

Jean was as good as her word. So successful had she been in selling the idea to Ford, senior, that Hertford had good news when he and Phyllis retired to their room next evening.

"Do you know what my Da told me in the yard today?" Hertford was full of it.

"He said he would help us to build and start up our own chicken house. AND that he would give us a site in the corner of the field at the top of the lane, to build a bungalow on."

Hertford's parents kept their promise.

They encouraged their son and daughter-in-law in every possible way they could, in the building and equipping of their chicken house.

This was stage number one of their scheme.

On 1st December, 1986, the first day-old chicks were delivered to the house. There were twenty thousand of them. They just appeared like fluffy yellow heaving masses as they clustered around the heaters, chirping away.

The clean smell of the fresh shavings and the continual cheeping of the birds, brought a sense of satisfaction to Hertford and Phyllis.

This was their first independent business venture. They hoped it would be successful.

December brought another milestone in the life of the family.

Another Christmas. What a thrill it was that year!

Now that Hertford and Phyllis had embarked upon the chicken house project, they had been forced to think outside themselves, and had come to terms, fully, with their family circumstances.

Wendsley was as precious now as their other two sons.

Three boys! More toys! Much noise!

Fantastic.

Hertford and Phyllis, Ford and Jean, had a busy but most rewarding Christmas. They all realised that if all went well with the business-to-bungalow-enterprise, then they might not be living together under the same roof next Christmas.

Everyone had mixed feelings about that.

In late January, 1987, the first crop of chickens were sold out of the chicken house. This was encouraging. Their first financial return.

So far, so good.

Then, on Friday 13th February, Hertford and Phyllis watched, with their two older sons, as another memorable event, for them, took place.

The diggers moved in to clean and level the site for their new bungalow.

Things were looking up.

Well done to the chicken house!

Its next batch of chickens would soon arrive!

CHAPTER TWELVE

Bleepers, Buggies and Builders

✚ ✚ ✚

"Beep! Beep! Beep!"

The big yellow bus from the Education and Library Board was by now coming each weekday morning, to take Thomas to School. He had been enrolled in a Special Care School in Lurgan, and became so excited when he heard the bleeper sounding.

Arms and legs were waved in enthusiasm, but in no particular order, when the bus began to reverse up the farm yard, right to the back door.

His daily attendance at school proved to be a double benefit to Phyllis. It gave her more time to concentrate on Ford and Wendsley, whilst it was comforting to realise that Thomas was under the supervision of experts who were equipped to care for both his physical and educational needs.

From the time that the walls of their new bungalow-to-be began to rise slowly out of the muddy ground, Phyllis liked to make a daily visit to the site.

It was lovely on a spring morning. The daffodils along the lane were in full bloom again and the birds sang and built their nests.

The increasing warmth of the sun, when it shone, and the gradual growth of a new home for the family, brought an increased optimism to the young wife an mother.

Winter was over once more.

A sense of things-aren't-that-bad-after-all swathed her soul.

Often, on fine days, with Thomas at School, and Hertford at work on the farm or in the chicken house, Phyllis would make a pilgrimage to the building site.

Such journeys required much effort.

She set off from the farmhouse with the two younger boys with her. One before and one behind.

Wendsley sat in the double buggy, specially bought for both Thomas and he.

There were two big problems with pushing that buggy.

Number one was the roughness of the lane. Potholes, centre-grass and large jagged stones didn't make for easy buggy-pushing.

The second problem was in the design of the buggy itself.

Particularly, the wheels. They were of 'the supermarket trolley' variety. All four of them walloped about independently, each one seeming to want to go in a direction of its own. None of them, however, seemed to have any inclination whatsoever, to go in the same direction as Phyllis!

Not only did she have to push on that lane, but Phyllis had to pull as well!

Besides grasping the handle of the buggy, her right hand had a rope wound around it. This rope, in turn, was attached to a blue ride-on toy tractor with the name 'Ford' emblazoned on the side of it. Perched astride his own 'personalised' tractor was Ford himself, aged two.

Although it required a lot of effort from Phyllis, this arrangement worked very well. Very well, that is, as long as Ford stayed on the tractor!

However, all it required was for him to spot a bee on a flower or a frog on the lane. Then he was away to investigate.

He just hopped off the tractor with no advance warning! Two things could happen as a result of this.

The tow-line could give a jerk and the tractor fall on its side and slither either to a dusty or a muddy halt, depending on the type of day it happened to be. That was the more preferable option.

The alternative occurred when Phyllis had worked up a bit of speed with her combination. In such an instance, when Ford skipped off, the tractor came lunging forward with such force that it hit his unsuspecting mother on the back of the legs!

Despite these minor trials, Phyllis made many journeys up that lane that spring.

A very pleasant spring gave way to a hot summer. As the bungalow began to take shape as a habitable form of a structure, the visits became more frequent.

The thirteenth of July was a holiday. A holiday for everyone, it seemed, except Hertford and his brother-in-law, Estlin. The pair of them spent that beautiful sunny day climbing ladders, stacking tiles on the roof.

School was finished by now, so all three of the children watched at various stages during the day as father and uncle toiled away. Up and down. Up and down.

Onto the roof with a pile of tiles. Then down the ladder, to wipe the brow and have a drink.

Then, onto the roof with a pile of tiles ...

Hertford and Phyllis, like so many who are eagerly watching a house being built, felt that when the roof was on, the bungalow was almost finished.

It didn't turn out that way.

There was a lot of fitting out to done.

Their small cottage-type bungalow had to have the Arnold trademark. An Aga in the kitchen.

There was one special feature of that bungalow which made it different from all the others of its size and type in the countryside at that time.

It had a ramp at the back door.

In late summer, and on into autumn, the whole family used to go up the lane, to explore the shell of their home-to-be.

Hertford and Phyllis moved from room to room, clearing up what they could, and planning what furniture they would have in each room and where it would be placed. These plans sometimes changed about three times a week!

Ford loved the empty echo of the rooms. He often stomped about, making as much noise as possible and laughing heartily. Then he would change the mood and creep about as quietly as he could, hiding from his mum and dad.

Thomas and Wendsley sat side by side in their twin buggy. The crackle of their laughter reverberated around the vacant rooms.

The family were so close. Being together. Working together. Laughing together.

It was a super time for all of them.

Fitting out slowed down in the winter months and Hertford concentrated his efforts on the chicken house, which was proving to be a success. It was a profitable concern, making money slowly but steadily, not perhaps as rapidly as Phyllis and Hertford had imagined, or would have liked.

The spring of 1988 was spent on the finishing touches. When Phyllis made her trips to the new bungalow, it was to work. In earnest.

There was brushing up, rubbing down, and scrubbing out to be done.

There was painting, papering and polishing to be done.

Monday 6th June, 1988, was moving day. It began as any other term-time weekday would have done.

Beep! Beep! Up the yard. The bus arrived and took Thomas off to school.

Then the flit began, for real. There was no massive removal van required here. No gang of men. Not on a farm did you need that kind of service.

The removal vehicle was a tractor and horse box. The removal team consisted of Hertford, his father and his brother Tyrrell.

Back and forward, back and forward, up and down the lane they went.

Pothole-puddle-water splashed away from the wheels of the tractor and horse box. It was a warm but overcast day. There were occasional heavy showers.

The flitting turned out to be a coats-on, coats-off, try-not-to-let-the-stuff-get-wet kind of an operation.

As the items were brought into the bungalow one by one, Phyllis directed the 'removal men' where to place them.

Wendsley sat in his buggy taking it all in, shaking his rattles, and generally enjoying himself.

Ford occupied himself by riding up and down on the tractor and running from room to room, getting amongst everybody's feet and generally enjoying himself.

Eventually everything was moved in.

Now all it required was for everybody to be moved in. They weren't going to have long to wait for that either.

When Wendsley began to kick and squeal they all knew that the time was fast approaching. He had heard the big yellow bus coming. The bleeper was going outside.

Thomas would soon be home.

When Phyllis opened the door to go out she was followed by Ford, who suddenly passed her and dashed forward.

He climbed up into the bus and found where Thomas was sitting in his chair. Then he helped the driver to remove the straps which held the chair in place.

When the chair was lowered from the bus, Phyllis pushed her eldest son up the specially designed ramp, and into their new home.

Thomas had left for school from his granny's house, and had come home to his own.

Now they were complete as a family in their new home. Granda Arnold and Tyrrell had left. There were just the five of them, with their own roof over their heads, at last.

Phyllis sat down in the living room, amongst the soon-to-be-cleared-up-clutter and gathered the three boys around her.

Thomas and Wendsley were in the double buggy. She held Ford gently with a restraining arm.

Then she thanked God, audibly, for their new home and for the husband and family she had.

"Thank You, Lord," she said, "for this lovely new bungalow. Thank You for Hertford and Thomas, for Ford and Wendsley. Come and share our new home with us. Help us all to be happy here. Thank You again, Lord. Amen."

Hertford saw his wife, with their boys around her, and heard her prayer.

He just granted her 'a fool's pardon'.

But he said nothing.

Although this kind of religious thing never did any good, he reasoned, it couldn't do much harm.

Now, could it?

But it pleased Phyllis. It afforded her a sense of peace. She just had to acknowledge the goodness of her God, Who had been so patient with her for so long.

The ice had melted further.

She had taken God under her notice once more.

She was on her way back.

Again.

CHAPTER THIRTEEN

Work, Whistle and Work

✤ ✤ ✤

The summer of 1988 saw the Arnold family settle happily into their new bungalow.

Now that the school holidays had arrived, Phyllis used to take the three boys around to her parents home often. Nana and Papa Blakely loved to see their grandchildren.

Hertford was usually hard at work. He had to be, but he liked to be. He had no choice, but he didn't care. It gave him a sense of satisfaction to provide for his family.

Papa took a particular interest in Thomas. He would have Thomas sitting beside him in his special chair, and he would talk to him, laugh with him and generally keep him amused. His most unique achievement, however, and therefore the one which gave him greatest pleasure, was that he taught Thomas to whistle.

They used to sit side by side for long periods and Papa would whistle a few notes to Thomas. When his young grandson laughed and gurgled, Papa continued the performance.

Then, after a few weeks of whistling enjoyment, Papa was absolutely delighted to see Thomas, who would never be able to speak, try to purse his lips to imitate him.

Fantastic incentive for further effort!

Finally, the big day came!

The day when Thomas actually made a noise!

Thomas startled himself! He was so thrilled when he realised that he could make some sort of a sound, that he did it over and over again. The more excited he became, though, the less control he had, and his attempts ended in soundless sucks and blows.

Gradually, over a number of visits, Papa taught his grandson to control his cheek and mouth movements and the whistling improved.

When Papa asked Thomas to show everybody what a clever boy he was and how he could whistle, it was often difficult to determine who was the more pleased. Thomas the whistler, or Papa the tutor!

September was back to School month.

The big yellow bus with the big noisy bleeper had returned to the front of the bungalow for Thomas.

Ford started in Nursery School, and his Granda Arnold made it his special responsibility to transport his young namesake to School.

Phyllis settled into an autumn routine of housework, shopping, and taking Wendsley to his physiotherapy classes in Craigavon Hospital.

As for Hertford, he just worked and worked and worked.

Cash flow had become a problem. The main trouble was that there seemed to be more cash flowing out than there was flowing in.

Their difficulty was not uncommon to young couples with young families.

It was called, 'making ends meet'.

Two crops of chickens had been sold out of the chicken house that autumn but they hadn't been as profitable as Hertford and Phyllis had planned.

They could live off the chicken house.

Yes. Certainly.

But they couldn't buy anything extra!

No curtains. No carpets. No luxuries.

To augment their income, Hertford took on yet more work. He used his father's power hose and went around local farms hosing down haysheds, cattle sheds, silos. Anywhere, indeed, where cleaning was needed and money could be made.

Christmas 1988 was, as usual, a blissful together-time for them all. They were now in their own home and at their own fireside. They had their own Christmas dinner in the oven of the Aga in the kitchen, and their own Christmas tree in the corner of the living room. Cosy.

Of necessity, however, the Christmas holiday period was short. None of these Christmas-to-New-Year combined vacations for Hertford.

He was back out and on to a bungalow roof, hosing down the tiles, in the chill of December 27th, the day after Boxing Day.

With all of Hertford's endeavours, on the farm, in the chicken house and with the power hose, the situation began to improve.

Things were looking more hopeful. Chinks of light were beginning to appear in the financial murk.

Still, there were things which Phyllis felt she wanted.

There were even things that she was convinced they needed.

But the cold stark reality was that they just couldn't afford them. And wouldn't be able to, for some time to come.

She felt that with Hertford working so hard, she also should be doing her bit for the furnishing fund. Pulling her weight.

But what could a young mother, with three children all under five years of age, and two of them handicapped into the bargain, do?

Well, what?

CHAPTER FOURTEEN

No Trifling Matter

❖ ❖ ❖

It was February 1989. Tea-time, late one afternoon.

Phyllis was spoon-feeding Thomas and Wendsley, alternately, as they sat in their high-chairs. The chairs were placed two yards apart, and Phyllis sat between them, feeding the boys from trifles which she had bought in Marks and Spencers.

Her two sons absolutely loved these smooth desserts. Phyllis appreciated them too for the simple reason that the boys were so fond of them, and that they didn't have to be mashed, strained or pureed.

Suddenly a thought came to her. It was so obvious that she was surprised that she hadn't thought of it before.

I could make those trifles, she reckoned. No problem. All I would need would be some cake, some fruit, some jelly, some custard ... Easily obtained ingredients. I could stop and start when I had the time. It would certainly be simpler than trying to bake stuff in the Aga ...

That was it! Trifles. Desserts.

When Hertford came up for his tea, about an hour later, his wife was so enthusiastic about this "great idea", this "flash of inspiration", which she had just had.

"I know now what I could do, Hertford," she began eagerly. "To make a little bit of extra money, you know."

Hertford smiled wryly. He was ever so slightly cynical. He was used to these bright ideas. Phyllis had been going to raise bedding plants one week, fatten turkeys the next week, and bake apple tarts the next!

"Well, what is it now?" he asked, resignedly, as he sat down at the end of the table.

"I would like to start making trifles. Desserts, you know, Hertford, in the house. Thomas and Wendsley love them, we are spending a fortune on them, I could easily make them, and what the boys couldn't eat, I could sell"

When her husband paused from his eating to comment, it was to dismiss the whole idea with a we-have-heard-it-all-before type reply.

"Have you no wit, Phyllis?" he asked, jokingly. He was mildly amused by all these harebrained schemes. None of them ever came to anything.

"Think now. How could you cope with all that?" he went on.

"Think of all the stuff you would need. And there are the three boys to be looked after. Wendsley has to be taken to physiotherapy. Don't be daft, Phyllis. Give yourself a break."

A sweeping wave of Hertford's arm across the table accompanied his final pronouncement. With that gesture he consigned the entire pudding project to the mists of oblivion, where it would join a dozen or so other nonstarters.

Phyllis wasn't going to be that easily put off.

This was a good one. She knew it. Not like the dried flowers or the buns-in-boxes.

She didn't sleep very soundly that night.

There were plans to be made. Amounts of ingredients to be calculated. A time-table to be sorted out.

Next morning was a school morning.

Thomas went off in the big yellow bus, and Granda Arnold called for Ford, and whisked him away to Nursery School.

When she saw Hertford safely dispatched to the chicken house, and Wendsley secured in the buggy, Phyllis got out the Yellow Pages.

Having found the heading she was looking for 'Packaging Materials' she ran her finger down the list. After biro-marking a few of the most promising looking companies, she started to make the calls.

"Hello," she would begin. "I was wondering do you sell those little round plastic containers that would hold a small dessert?"

If the answer was "Yes," then she would continue, "Well, could I buy fifty of them from you?"

It was probably a good job Phyllis couldn't see the face at the other end of the phone. She could only hear the voice, which was invariably polite.

"I'm sorry, Madam," would come the reply, time-and-time again. "The minimum quantity we can supply is one thousand."

A thousand! A thousand!

"What on earth would I do with a thousand of those wee tub things?" she asked herself.

After the fourth or fifth phone call she gave up and had a good laugh about it. She could see a funny side to the whole operation.

Phyllis had a vision of trifles on the kitchen bench, trifles on the kitchen table. trifles on the windowsill ...

The twin buggy could become an unapproachable island, marooned in a sea of trifles on the kitchen floor ...

There must be another way. There must be somebody who could help her. She wasn't going to give up. Surely not everybody in the whole wide world sold their trifle tubs by the thousand.

Then she remembered.

There was a fruit and vegetable shop in Lurgan where she had seen small trifles in small plastic pots. Two things she recalled about them.

They were decorated with 'hundreds and thousands' and they only appeared on Saturday mornings.

Phyllis knew the greengrocer well. She brought her fruit and vegetables from him sometimes.

Here was someone whom she was sure could help her, and she reckoned that she knew him well enough to solicit his help.

It was worth a try.

Sure enough, her next call was to prove more productive. Having explained her need, she found her greengrocer friend to be most accommodating.

"No trouble at all, Phyllis," he replied. "Come on in here any time and I will get you sorted out."

As Phyllis was fired with enthusiasm to see this project "off the ground" as soon as possible, she decided to go straight away. There's no time like the present, when there is something pressing to be done!

The benevolent vegetable vendor supplied her with ten dozen trifle tubs. Any less, he figured wouldn't be worth melting a jelly for.

On the way home from Lurgan with Wendsley in his special car seat, Phyllis stopped at a supermarket. There was shopping to be done.

She bought tins of custard, packets of jelly crystals, tins of fruit, packets of trifle sponges and two large containers of fresh cream.

Now she had both the ingredients and the inspiration. All she needed was the time.

When Hertford came in for his lunch he was thirsty. He nearly always was. Chicken houses were dry, stuffy places.

On opening the fridge to help himself to a drink he stepped back in mock amazement. It was a little bit melodramatic, his watching wife thought.

"What in the name of the world is all this, Phyllis?" he enquired, with a sardonic smile. "Are we having visitors tonight or something? Somebody you haven't told me about?"

Totally disregarding his comment, and while he unceremoniously rearranged the fridge in search of a drink, the longsuffering Phyllis set about explaining to him the purpose of it all.

"No, Hertford. You remember I told you that I would like to have a go at making some trifles. Well, what you see in there are the ingredients for them."

After lunch Hertford rose from the table.

Approaching the back door he couldn't resist the temptation to poke a bit more fun at his zealous wife.

"Make sure you call me in when the trifles are ready," he quipped.

Phyllis laughed. "Keep you quiet and get back out into that yard again," she retorted.

Her husband took the hint, and went.

With Hertford back to his work, Phyllis was now in a position to start hers.

She worked hard.

By the time the bleeper sounded, and Thomas returned, she had the bases for six dozen trifles made, and sitting in orderly rows on a big white tray. She put them into the fridge to set, planning that when tea was over, and the boys were in bed, she would complete them.

It didn't work out that way. There just wasn't the time.

Not to be deterred, Phyllis rose at six a.m. next morning, put custard and fresh cream on her six dozen trifles, and returned them to the fridge.

When Thomas and Ford had gone off to their different schools, Phyllis fastened Wendsley into his seat in the back of the car. Then she opened the boot.

As she struggled out of the front door with her big flat tray of trifles, all neatly arranged in regimental rows, Hertford came dandering up from the chicken house.

"And where, might I ask, would you be heading to at this hour of the morning?" he enquired.

Phyllis knew that he knew where she was hoping to go, but just in case he should be left in any doubt, she replied, "I am going to see if I can sell these trifles."

"Who are you going to ask? Did you ring some shopkeepers? You are not just going to carry that tray into a supermarket somewhere and shout, "Who will buy my lovely trifles?"

Hertford was not being very successful at disguising his mixed feelings.

He loved his wife. What was more, he admired his wife. He appreciated her industry, and understood her reason for doing what she was doing.

He was just afraid, however, that she was going to make a real 'pig's ear' of herself.

"No. I didn't ring anybody, but I will sell all of these. Every single one of them. You'll see," his wife responded, with apparent confidence.

She too was engaged in a cover-up job. How she wished that the words of her mouth were expressing the real sentiments of her heart.

But they weren't

Deep down there was this niggling fear.

There would be a lot of eating, and selling, in six dozen trifles. Seventy-two.

Where would she find anybody wanting to buy seventy-two home-made trifles?

CHAPTER FIFTEEN

Sold Out

✦ ✦ ✦

As Phyllis drove up the lane towards the main road that morning, she prayed.

"Lord, please guide me. Direct me to where to go with these trifles. I need to sell them, but I don't know where to start."

Stopping at the end of the lane she was in a quandary.

"Should I go right? Or should I go left?"

She just wasn't sure.

After a momentary pause, Phyllis decided that she would go round to her parent's house. That would be a good place to begin. If her daddy liked them that would always be a start!

As she drove along she was conscious of Wendsley kicking the back of her seat. He loved the car. The crows of his laughter cheered his mother. Made her feel that this was going to be a worthwhile jaunt.

When Phyllis arrived in the farmyard of her parents' home at Gracehall, near Dollingstown, her father and mother were out and about. They were going about their early morning must-be-done-daily farm duties.

Both of them approached the car, each from a different angle.

Her mother appeared slightly concerned.

"My goodness, Phyllis, you are up early this morning. Is anything wrong? Where are you off to?" Ethel Blakely enquired.

Tom, her father, peered into the back seat. When he had assured himself that everything was normal, he spoke in to Wendsley.

"Hello there, my wee son," he began. "Where's your bottle today?"

As well as teaching Thomas to whistle, the boys' granda derived particular pleasure from another of his achievements.

He had taught both Thomas and Wendsley to hold their own feeding bottles. This proved to be a great help to their mum, for it meant that the boys could take their own drinks. It was no mean feat either, considering the very limited co-ordination that the boys had of their limb movements.

It was the fruit of hours of loving and painstaking labour.

Phyllis got out of the car and smiled at them both.

"No, there's nothing the matter, don't worry," she assured them. "I just wanted to show you something."

With that she flicked open the boot. There, carefully packed on their big flat tray, were six dozen dainty trifles.

Her parents just gazed in wonder for a moment.

"Where are you going to with these, Phyllis? Where did you get them anyway?" her mother asked at length.

"Look mummy," Phyllis replied, "I didn't get them anywhere. I made them and now I am going to try to sell them. But I wanted daddy and you to be the first to taste them. Away down to the house there and get a couple of spoons would you?"

As her mother went down to the house to fetch the spoons, Tom chuckled to himself.

"What will you be at next, Phyllis?" he laughed. He had heard Hertford poke gentle fun at some of his daughter's get-rich-quick ideas, now and then.

When the spoons arrived, Tom and Ethel were invited to take their pick of the desserts. As they ate, Phyllis explained.

"I took a notion to make these trifles for three reasons. Firstly, the boys love them, so I'm having to buy them. Secondly, I can make them at home in my own time, and then hopefully I can sell a few of them to make an extra pound or two. Help us to buy one or two little extras for the bungalow, if you know what I mean."

By the time Phyllis had finished her explanation, her dad had almost finished his dessert. He scraped and scraped at the bottom of the little plastic tub, in case he would miss some. When he was sure there was absolutely nothing left he placed the spoon in the container and made to hand it back to Phyllis.

As he did so he gave the final verdict.

"That was really delicious, Phyllis," he said.

"Take another one there if you like," invited Phyllis.

Her dad didn't need to be told twice. When he had repossessed his spoon he did just that!

When the score in trifles was, Dad two, Mum one, Phyllis prepared to get back into the car to rejoin Wendsley who had been watching the proceedings out through the window.

"If you don't sell them Phyllis, bring them back here and I will buy the whole job lot from you," her father promised.

His promise was a measure of both her parents' appreciation of their daughter's handiwork.

As she waved goodbye and drove away, Phyllis consulted her Heavenly Navigator again.

"Where now, Lord?" she enquired. "Where next?"

Her Lord was expected to be a signpost. A leaning-post. But always and only as a last resort. And always and only when it suited Phyllis.

On her way back to Donacloney she stopped at three grocery shops.

She didn't need to go any further.

Her Lord, her Guide, her last-ditch Leader, had prepared her customers and directed her car.

In those first three shops, her first three calls, Phyllis sold all sixty-nine remaining trifles.

She drove home with a light heart. As Wendsley chortled away in the back seat she glanced at him every so often in the rear view mirror.

He was happy.

She was happy.

It was great.

But would Hertford be happy? Would he even believe her?

When the car pulled up at the front of the bungalow, Hertford appeared as if from nowhere. He had been secretly, almost anxiously, awaiting their return.

Trying again to mask his concern with a wisecrack, he asked, "Well, what is it for lunch. Trifles, I suppose?"

Phyllis was smiling as she helped her husband to unbuckle the straps around Wendsley's car seat.

"No, Hertford. I'm sorry it won't be trifles today." she replied. Hertford set off towards the house carrying Wendsley. Taking out the empty tray she followed him in.

While Hertford installed Wendsley in his high-chair in the kitchen, Phyllis rather deliberately propped the tray against a table leg beside him.

Her husband got the message, but he still had to ask the question.

"You didn't sell them all did you?" he asked, almost incredulously.

"Yes, Hertford, I sold every single one of them. Didn't I tell you I would? And what's more I only visited three shops!" Phyllis retorted.

Two things she omitted to tell him, though. She didn't dare confess to her mental misgivings prior to her selling expedition, or to the fact that she had prayed to her Lord for guidance.

Indeed in all the excitement she had even forgotten to whisper a 'Thank You' to Him.

Over lunch much lively discussion took place. Where Phyllis had been. What the people had said. How much the trifles had sold for. These and many other topics were gone into.

Hertford just couldn't hear enough.

Shortly after two o'clock when he had returned, rather reluctantly, back out to work, the phone rang.

"Phyllis, is that you?" the voice at the other end of the line had a request. "Could you bring us some more of those wee dessert things tomorrow? We are sold out already today?"

"I could certainly," Phyllis was happy to respond. "I will have them with you tomorrow morning."

When the two boys had come home from school, Phyllis found Hertford in the yard.

"I have to go to the shops for more stuff, Hertford," she told him. "I will take the three boys with me."

So when she had the three of them all safely belted into their seats in the car, Phyllis set off. To buy yet more jellies, custard, trifle sponges, tinned fruit, cream ...

After watching the car speed away up the lane, Hertford decided that it was coffee-time. He would go into the house and make himself a cup.

While he sat idly by the table, sipping his coffee and staring at the empty tray, the phone rang again. It was five-past-four.

"Is Phyllis there?" came the query.

"No. I'm sorry she's not," Hertford replied. "She's away out to do some shopping. Can I take a message?"

"Yes. I'm sure you could," the caller continued. "Just ask her to bring us a couple of dozen more of those trifles tomorrow, if she could. They have been very popular today. We are sold out already."

"No problem. That will be O.K. I will tell her when she gets back," Hertford assured the shopkeeper.

When they had said their "Goodbyes" he replaced the receiver.

Now he was convinced.

These trifles were going to take off after all.

The joking was over.

He wouldn't, he couldn't make fun of Phyllis any more.

She was on to a winner this time!

CHAPTER SIXTEEN

Do You Want A Job?

✦ ✦ ✦

The end of June brought two added pressures for Phyllis and her trifle tub turnout. They were pleasant problems to have, but required careful planning.

Firstly, Thomas and Ford were commencing their summer holiday from school. All three boys were pleased about that.

The two older boys were happy to be at home, and Wendsley was glad of the company.

Then with the better weather, and glowing word-of-mouth recommendation, the orders for trifles increased steadily.

To see everything done that had to be done in any one day, a routine had to be established.

It was most important.

Those summer mornings began early.

When Hertford rose at six-o-clock to go down to attend to the chickens, Phyllis also rose and brought the three children down into the living room.

One by one she changed, dressed, and fed them. This was a time-consuming operation.

After Ford, who was now over four years of age, had eaten his breakfast, he became guardian of his brothers, one older and other younger, than himself.

Phyllis laid Thomas and Wendsley on the living-room floor with their bottles, which they had learnt to hold for themselves, thanks to the untiring efforts of Papa Blakely.

As Ford sat on the floor on his knees, watching the early morning children's T.V. programmes, he would hear a clunk. That was a bottle down. Occasionally, and especially when the bottles were full and heavy, one of the boys would drop his. Thomas and Wendsley could hold their bottles up, but they couldn't pick them up.

Ungrudgingly, Ford would leave off his viewing, retrieve the dropped bottle, and replace it in welcoming hands. He would then return to his knees before the T.V. and resume where he left off.

That was, of course, until the next clunk ...

Shortly after eight a.m. Hertford would come up for his breakfast.

When breakfast was all over and cleared away, Phyllis set to work on the desserts.

The utility room now housed two tall white fridges. Phyllis spent the morning preparing the bases for the day's trifles. Sponge, jelly and fruit were all added to the tubs which she had arranged on trays.

These were then returned to the fridge to set.

Then came a break for family lunch. This was a happy sharing time. Hertford came in for lunch and helped his wife with the boys, playing with them, feeding them, settling them.

After lunch was white coat time. When Hertford had showered, he donned a white coat and hat and helped Phyllis to put the finishing touches to the trifles.

Custard had to be added. There was cream to be whipped and spread on them. Finally, the decoration had to be done.

Before delivery, the lids were put in place. The original Phyllis trifles didn't have lids, but now that she was confident enough to order her tubs by the thousand, she was supplied with see-through lids as well! And they even stretched to labels!

August was progressing, business was buzzing, the green blackberries had started to turn red on the lane and every draper's shop in Lurgan had a "Back to School" poster in the window, when the phone rang one afternoon.

Phyllis was out. Hertford answered.

He was pleased with the call. He was sure Phyllis would be too. It could be their big break.

Hertford thought that his wife was never going to come back. He was growing more impatient with every passing minute for he so much wanted to see her face when he told her the news.

When she did return, it wasn't long until her husband told her of his telephone conversation of an hour or so earlier.

"There was a man rang there a while ago," Hertford began, trying to hide his own excitement behind a-matter-of-fact voice. "A distributor he calls himself. He has what he describes as a "chilled run". That means that he supplies small shops and service stations and places like that with chilled goods. He has obviously seen our stuff out there somewhere for he wants to know if we could supply him."

Phyllis stopped dead in the middle of her back-home-again rush around.

"I don't believe you!" was her instant reply. She was used to Hertford and his antics.

She was sure he was winding her up! A friendly April-fool-in-August leg-pull.

"O.K. So you don't believe me," Hertford continued. "I was pretty sure you wouldn't anyway. Well, just to prove that it's right, there's his number. He is waiting for you to ring him up."

Having been convinced by the number scrawled on the back of an envelope, Phyllis did as she was asked.

She rang him up.

It was genuine! She heard the same request that Hertford had heard just a little over an hour before.

"I have seen your wee desserts, Mrs Arnold," the caller explained. "I like the look of them. Well made and tastefully presented. Think they would be good sellers. Any chance of calling round to see you later on tonight? Say about nine o'clock or so?"

Phyllis did a spot of quick thinking.

Chickens, changing, feeding, bottles, bedtime.

Nine o'clock.

They could just about make it.

"Yes. That will be fine. Nine o'clock would probably suit us well," she agreed.

Then she replaced the receiver and flew into a flat spin!

When the businessman arrived, a few minutes after nine o'clock, there wasn't a bottle, a nappy, a rattle or a squeaky toy in sight!

Couldn't give the man the wrong impression! He might think that they couldn't cope with his order!

In general conversation, after the usual weather-type openers, the prospective customer asked a number of questions. He was curious about this apparently very efficient outfit.

"Why did you think of doing desserts?" he wanted to know. That, and the next few like, "How did you start up?" and, "Who all do you supply?" were easy. Hertford and Phyllis were pleased to present him with all the information he wanted.

Then came the big one. The one they had been waiting for.

"Would you supply me?" the distributor enquired.

"Well how many would you be talking about?" Phyllis was anxious to know. It would be important to find out what the phrase "supply me" actually entailed.

"I would need twenty dozen a night, for four nights of the week," came the immediate response.

The chilled goods vendor had done his homework. He knew exactly how many he needed.

Phyllis swallowed hard.

Twenty dozen a night, four nights a week.

Hertford and she were at that time producing thirty dozen trifles a week for distribution to thirteen different outlets. They were finding that workload tough, the schedule tight.

Now here was a man, sitting there at their table asking for eighty dozen trifles a week for himself! One customer. One outlet. Nearly three times their total current production level.

Thirty dozen for their present customers.

Eighty dozen for their new one.

One hundred and ten dozen trifles in a week.

Well over a thousand!

No funny fantasies here. This was for real!

While Phyllis was juggling with her mental arithmetic she was acutely aware of her husband. Hertford was running his fingers through his hair, rolling his eyes, and shuffling uncomfortably.

Their eyes met across the table.

Before Hertford could open his mouth to say, "There's no way, boy, we could do the like of that," he had sustained a hearty kick on the shin!

Phyllis had the situation under control.

"That will be all right," she assured her customer-to-be. "We can manage that O.K."

"Mind you I don't want to be let down." The businessman was just a little concerned. "I can't afford to be let down," he went on.

He hoped that he wasn't asking for more than this hardworking couple in their nice new bungalow could cope with.

"Don't you worry," Phyllis declared confidently. "If we take it on, and we will, then we won't let you down. We have been thinking for some time that we will need to recruit a bit of extra help. Your order has confirmed that for us. We will have to think about it soon."

Hertford hadn't realised that he had been thinking seriously about taking on somebody else to work for them, but he didn't even open his eyes wide in amazement. And he certainly knew not to say anything.

The thought of a second black-and-blue shin put that notion out of his head!

The chilled-food-run-man went away satisfied, and he had hardly reached the end of the lane when Hertford and Phyllis set about planning a totally revised daily routine.

The last week of August was to be the first week of the new orders.

It turned out to be chaotic. Crazy.

Hertford and Phyllis were flopping into bed late and crawling out of it again early. They had to honour all their normal commitments and they had promised that they wouldn't let their newest customer down.

They didn't either. Not once.

But the trifles were taking their toll.

In time. And in temper.

There was only a certain amount of this that any human being could stick.

The return of Thomas and Ford to school in September eased the pressure a little.

Phyllis worked all morning in the utility room with Wendsley sitting in his buggy tilted into a backward position in the doorway. He just loved to watch all that was going on. His mum made sure that he felt part of it. She would chat away to him as she worked, and he would respond with contented gurgles. Then, in the late morning, he would fall asleep and have a doze until lunchtime.

Meanwhile, Hertford was rushing about his farm work to return to the bungalow as soon as possible. When he was duly washed and changed he busied himself with the trifles as well.

They couldn't go on working this hard. They knew it.

Something would have to happen. Or something was going to give. It just couldn't continue.

On a Wednesday morning in early September, Phyllis had a telephone call from her sister.

After a few minutes of conversation Phyllis said to her, "Look, Heather, I hate to say this to you, but I am very sorry I haven't got time to talk to you now. I am up to my eyes here. There's jelly and fruit all over the place. I will give you a ring later on in the day. Probably this evening some time, when I get a minute."

Life for her sister was far from busy, however. She had just rung up for a chat. To pass a while of the morning.

"It's well for you, Phyllis," was Heather's immediate and honest reply. "You are lucky to be so busy. The two children are back to school, I have all the housework done and I'm bored stiff. And still it's only a quarter-past eleven in the morning."

Suddenly Phyllis had a brainwave. Another one.

"I tell you what, Heather," she suggested. "Why don't you put on your hat and coat and come round here. I will give you something to occupy your mind. I guarantee that I can stop you from thinking long."

Heather was delighted. She came round to the busy bungalow straight away.

Then she came the next morning at nine-thirty, after she had seen the children off to school. She left again at two-thirty to collect them to take them home.

She did the same on Friday …

Heather's assistance proved to be invaluable. She was keen, learnt quickly, and had the added advantage of knowing the family circumstances. With her around, Phyllis felt free to take Wendsley to physiotherapy or go into Lurgan to shop.

So much did Hertford and Phyllis value her assistance that they offered her a job.

Heather loved the work, and was pleased to accept, thus becoming Phyllis and Hertford's first permanent employee.

CHAPTER SEVENTEEN

Dreary Weather. Scary Word

✤ ✤ ✤

It was mid-November now. Dark, damp, foggy weather.

One Saturday afternoon Phyllis noticed that Thomas didn't appear to be very well. He and Wendsley had always been prone to colds and chest infections, so their mum was constantly aware of any change in their eating, sleeping, smiling, whistling pattern.

When afternoon became evening and the dark foggy day became a dark foggy night, Thomas seemed to be worse. Continuous coughing took so much out of him that it was painful to watch.

Hertford and Phyllis became really anxious. If this condition deteriorated any further it could result in Thomas being admitted to Hospital. It had done so on a number of previous occasions.

As it was Saturday evening, however, they decided to wait until Sunday morning to see if his cold would become even worse. They didn't want to trouble the doctor or anyone else unnecessarily.

On Sunday morning there was no doubt about what course of action they should take.

Thomas had grown steadily worse through the night. His coughing had become hard and heavy. His breathing was becoming laboured. It was obviously time for the doctor. No question about that.

After examining the sick child the doctor advised that Thomas be admitted to Craigavon Hospital immediately.

Hertford's mother, Jean, took care of Ford and Wendsley while Hertford and Phyllis took Thomas into Hospital. It was always a relief Phyllis felt, to get him into Hospital. This was where he could be best cared for. This was where the experts were.

When Thomas had been settled into bed, Tom and Ethel Blakely came up to visit their little grandson.

The grandparents both found something to please them. Something to take away with them. A straw of hope to which they could cling, desperately.

"He can't be too bad if he can ..."

Nana Blakely was pleased that Thomas had drunk a bottle of milk. That could only be a good sign.

Papa was pleased that through his weakness and coughing Thomas had even made an attempt to whistle! When Papa whistled softly to him, he made every effort to respond. But it was difficult.

Breath was in short supply.

When the grandparents had gone home, just ever so slightly more content, Hertford and Phyllis stayed with Thomas until ten o'clock in the evening. Then they thought it best to go home, for a number of reasons.

Jean had been very good at caring for the other two boys, but she couldn't keep them all night. Also, and very importantly, they wanted to spend some time with their other two younger sons as well.

That was nothing to how much Ford and Wendsley look forward to seeing their mum and dad!

Besides the family considerations there was a basic personal physical need.

Rest. Sleep.

Over the past two days they had been anxious, agitated. There hadn't been any time for a rest.

Now with Hertford and Phyllis consoling themselves that Thomas was "in the best place" perhaps they could snatch an hour or two's shut-eye

It didn't work out.

They went to bed, but not to sleep. It was so distressing.

Thomas was ill. Very ill. They both knew it, deep in their hearts. They had an empty feeling in the pit of the stomach.

They could close their eyes, but their brains wouldn't stop. Whirling on, throwing up thoughts, worries, ultimate consequences ...

Next morning Phyllis left home at seven o'clock to return to Craigavon Hospital. Hertford was left to feed Wendsley and do what he could on the trifle orders.

When she arrived at her sick son's bedside she realised that his condition had declined further. Now he just lay there, sleeping all the time.

Phyllis rubbed cream tenderly on his face. Then she combed his hair. She thought he was so lovely. She had done for him what any mother would have done for an ailing child. There was more that she would like to do, though.

It would be great to feed him. See him eat something.

When a nurse came into the ward she told Phyllis that Thomas wouldn't take his bottle at six o'clock. This was disturbing.

Hadn't her mother been so pleased yesterday because Thomas had been well enough to take his bottle?

"If you bring me a warm bottle with some Weetabix I will try to feed him," Phyllis volunteered. It would be great to actually DO something, rather than sit and gaze at Thomas, while listening to his laboured breathing.

The nurse duly brought a plate of Weetabix and some warm milk, which Phyllis tried to give to Thomas.

It was a fruitless effort.

Thomas just didn't respond, when his mum, with tears in her eyes and a tremble in her voice, begged, "Come on now, Thomas, son. Here's your breakfast. Take some of it for mummy."

No reaction. Not a movement. Not a flicker.

Nothing.

Just continued sleep.

Phyllis felt strange. It was as though her son, to whom she was so close, was now somehow far away. In some kind of different distant realm.

Shortly after ten o'clock the medical staff made a ward round. Phyllis spoke to one of the doctors, whom she knew.

"Doctor, Thomas won't make any attempt to eat or drink for me," she began, trying to be brave and hold back the tears. "He is not even interested in me being here. That is very peculiar. He just sleeps and sleeps and sleeps ..."

"Mrs Arnold, Thomas is very sick at the minute," the doctor replied, gently. "He can't keep getting better and coming home. His body is becoming very weak, and every one of these chesty attacks weakens it even more. The little body is just very, very tired."

Phyllis was beginning to get the message. It was filtering through to her brain, bit by bit.

When she had stepped out of that enveloping mist of the early morning and in through the Hospital door a few hours earlier, she had been strangely conscious of entering into a mist of a different kind.

She had changed from a wet clinging mist that made driving difficult to a weird psychological mist which totally obscured the future.

The mist in her mind was beginning to clear. And the shadowy shapes which she could just about glimpse through the gloom, her mind didn't dare to believe.

When the doctor had given her a few moments to come to terms with his first statement, he asked a question.

"Tell me, is Hertford coming up today?" he enquired.

"Yes he is," Phyllis replied. "He will be up later on."

"Well, I think you should ring him and ask him to get up here right away."

Although spoken with all the tenderness that the doctor could show there was a compelling urgency about the underlying message.

"We are going to put a drip up with Thomas for he is starting to dehydrate. Then we will be coming shortly to take him to have a chest x-ray."

The next stages of her son's treatment, though explained so kindly to Phyllis were lost on her.

She just wanted to find a telephone. To speak to her husband.

"Hertford, the doctor says that you should come up to the Hospital right away," she sobbed out. "Thomas is very bad."

When Hertford heard that message, he dropped all and drove to the Hospital, leaving his sister-in-law, Heather, to sort out dozens of trifles in various stages of preparation and to care for Wendsley.

At a quarter to eleven, Hertford arrived in the Hospital ward. As he and Phyllis sat by their son's bedside, he was very upset.

Leaning over the bed every now and again, Hertford would whisper softly, "Thomas, son, your mummy and daddy are here. Open your eyes son. Can you not hear me?"

No response. Never the slightest reaction.

Just continued restless sleep.

After lunchtime the nurses came and wheeled Thomas away for a chest x-ray. Within half-an-hour he was back again, lying in his bed. Still asleep.

Thomas had been back in the ward about an hour when a doctor came to the bedside.

"Could I speak to you both for a minute, Mr and Mrs Arnold?" he enquired.

When they had been shown into a little side room the doctor told them the news. It was the result of the x-ray.

"This is the worst we have ever seen Thomas," he began.

"Unfortunately, the x-rays show that both of his lungs are clouded over white with pneumonia."

What a shock! What a knockout blow!

"A chest infection," would have been easy. They had heard that often before. And coped.

But not this.

Pneumonia.

To Phyllis and Hertford this meant something different. There was a sickening final ring about it.

It was a scary, scary word.

Pneumonia.

CHAPTER EIGHTEEN

It Won't Be Long Now

✤ ✤ ✤

The remainder of that day was spent in a hazy blur of activity, then inactivity. Times of speaking to doctors, nurses and relatives who came and went noiselessly, like the fog. Then time of sitting in silent contemplation beside Thomas, holding his hand, putting cream on his face, combing his hair.

The medical staff asked Phyllis and Hertford if they would consider inviting their parents up to see Thomas, since he was so low. They did, and the distressed grandparents came.

Later that evening, a doctor spoke to Jean Arnold, Tom and Ethel Blakely, and Hertford and Phyllis as they were sitting together, in a state of stunned anxiety, in the ward.

"We have done all that we can for Thomas," he explained, quietly. "And we will continue to do everything possible from now on. Just at this minute though, there is little that we can do. The body is very, very weak. His condition is causing us some concern."

At midnight, Hertford and Phyllis went home. Papa Blakely insisted that he would stay all night and give them a chance to go home for a sleep.

When they arrived home Ford and Wendsley were in bed. They went to bed as well. But not to sleep.

How could they?

At six o'clock, on the morning of Tuesday 14th November, 1989, Hertford and Phyllis drove back to the Hospital again through dense pea-soup fog. Everything seemed to be closing in around them.

They relieved Papa Blakely who went off home for a few hours rest.

Thomas still lay there unmoving. Semi-conscious.

The morning dragged by.

Relatives came and went all morning, on padded pussy-feet, speaking in hushed whispers. It was as though they were afraid that they would waken Thomas - but how they wished that they could.

As Phyllis and Hertford's parents and brothers and sisters, one by one, made their entrance and exit, there was a flurry of medical activity.

Doctors entered and left the ward. They brought needles, charts, stethoscopes. Nurses changed the drip-feed bottles and checked the heart-monitor. Thomas had his chest sounded regularly.

Everything possible was being done for him. Just as the doctor had promised.

It was all go.

Then, just after lunch, and in startling contrast to the frenetic morning build-up, the fever of activity ceased. A quietness, a stillness, fell on the ward.

The two grandmothers made another brief visit. In and out again, soundlessly.

They came clutching damp crumpled handkerchiefs.

They left again clutching even damper crumpled handkerchiefs.

At a quarter to four in the afternoon, Hertford and Phyllis were alone in the ward with their very sick son. This was unusual, strange even, since there had been a constant coming and going of relatives all day. The relatives were still around the Hospital at various locations. They couldn't draw themselves away, but there weren't any of them in the ward at that precise time.

Thomas lay motionless on the bed, still in a semi-conscious state. He was perspiring freely. His hair was soaked in sweat. Phyllis leaned over, and with a mother's tender touch, dried his hair, face and neck occasionally. His face had become a peculiar grey-white colour. The line of his lips was barely distinguishable.

The only sound was the regular beat of the heart monitor.

Sister Mavis Brush slipped quietly into the ward. Hertford and Phyllis knew and respected Sister Brush. She had been ever so kind to them, and Thomas and Wendsley, on their regular visits to Craigavon Hospital.

After entering the ward, Sister Brush kept her two hands behind her, holding on to the handle of the door. She seemed almost reluctant to proceed any further into the ward. She had the look of someone who had something to say, but wasn't exactly sure of how to say it.

It was obvious that she had been weeping.

Having steadied herself by the door for a few minutes, she took a couple of steps forward into the ward. Towards the bed. Towards Thomas. Towards his distraught parents.

"I am going off duty now at four o'clock, Phyllis and Hertford," she began gently. "But I am going home to pray for you both, that God will be with you in what you are about to come through."

She paused for breath. The sister was taking her time, weighing her words carefully, speaking them compassionately.

"Thomas is very low at the moment. We have done everything in our power both physically and medically to keep him here. He is now barely clinging to life. But he is in the hands of the Lord. For some time now I have dreaded this moment ..."

There was a second pause. Longer this time. Hertford and Phyllis sat gazing at her. They were in a kind of daze, but they appreciated her genuine concern. Even Hertford didn't resent the reference to "the hands of the Lord". Here was a woman who felt deeply about what she was saying. He could take it from her. She lived it.

Fumbling in the pocket of her nurse's uniform, Mavis Brush produced a piece of folded paper. "For some weeks now I have had this poem," she explained, still holding the folded paper lightly in her right hand. "I feel led of the Lord to give it to you now."

With that she stepped forward and offered the paper to Phyllis. As the heart-broken mother reached up to accept it, Sister Brush kissed her lovingly, spontaneously, on the cheek.

"Is there anything, anything at all, I can do for you, Hertford and Phyllis?" she enquired, with great tenderness.

"Yes, Mavis, there is something you could do for me," replied Phyllis. "I would love to nurse Thomas again. Would that be possible do you think?"

"I can sort that out for you O.K." said the sister.

Then she gave the instructions. "Hertford, could you lift him out of the bed onto Phyllis's knee, after I switch off the monitor? I will wheel the drip trolley round."

When the bleeping of the monitor ceased there was silence. A deep, intimate silence. This was tender-together time.

Mavis put a blanket around Thomas's legs as he sat on his mother's knee. He was so pale. His breathing was very laboured.

The little body was worn out. Spent. Exhausted.

It had nothing left to fight back with.

Hertford rhythmically massaged his son's cold feet.

Sister Brush put her arms around both of them. She didn't say anything more. She was weeping unashamedly now.

After she had been gone about ten minutes, Phyllis interrupted their hushed nursing vigil by asking, more for something to say, than because she really wanted to know, "I wonder what this poem is about?"

Phyllis tried unsuccessfully to shake the page open. Hertford helped her to open it out, and laid it flat in the not-around-Thomas hand.

Cradling her extremely sick son with one loving arm, Phyllis read the poem silently.

TO ALL PARENTS

I'll lend you, for a little while, a child of mine, He said,
For you to love while he shall live, and mourn when he is dead,
It may be six or seven years, or twenty two or three,
But will you, till I call him back, take care of him for Me?
He'll bring his charms to gladden you, and should his stay be brief,
You'll have his lovely memories as solace for your grief,
I cannot promise he will stay, as all from Earth return,
But there are lessons taught down there I want this child to learn,
I've looked the wide world over in my search for teachers true,
And from the throngs that crowd life's lanes, I have selected you,
Now will you give him all your love - not think the labour vain,
Nor hate Me when I come to call to take him back again,
I fancied that I heard them say, "Dear Lord, Thy will be done",
For all the joy this child shall bring, the risk of grief we'll run,
We'll shower him with tenderness and love him while we may,
For the happiness we've known, forever grateful stay,
And should the angels call for him much sooner than we planned,
We'll brave the bitter grief that comes, and try to understand.

No wonder Sister Brush had considered it appropriate. And no wonder, also, that she had waited until now to present it, tearfully, to them.

"Well, what's it all about?" Hertford enquired. "You must have it all read by now."

Without answering, Phyllis began to read the poem aloud.

As she read it out to him, through her tears, the words of the first line seemed to linger with her throughout the whole poem.

"I'll lend you, for a little while ..."

"Lend you - lend you, lend you, lend, - lend - lend ..."

The whole theme of the thing was about a loan. A child on loan. Phyllis knew from her experience that the idea of a loan was that it must be paid back. Some how. Some time.

They had been privileged to be given Thomas on loan. What joy he had brought.

Now the loan period was over.

The repayment date had arrived.

God was about to reclaim His precious possession.

This was reality.

Would they be able "to brave the bitter grief that comes?"

And could they, would they, even try to understand?

At half-past four Phyllis thought that Thomas was just a little bit better. His breathing did not appear to be so laboured. Tufts of blond spiky hair were sticking out all over his head.

"Could you lift him back into the bed again, Hertford?" she asked her husband.

Just as Hertford was straightening the limp unconscious body of his oldest son in the bed, and Phyllis was smoothing the bedclothes and preparing to comb his hair yet again, Sister Brush re-entered the ward.

She hadn't gone home, obviously. She had grown to know Thomas and his devoted parents well over the past six years.

How could she possibly go home, have her tea and watch the T.V. leaving them in this heart-rending position?

When she had re-connected the heart monitor and checked the drip, the sister sounded her young patient's chest.

Hertford was on one side of the bed. Phyllis was on the other.

"It won't be long now," she said gently,. "His breathing is becoming very shallow. Hold on to his wee hand Phyllis. Hold on tight."

The parents didn't need to be told what "It" was, that wouldn't be long now. They knew. But they just couldn't believe it. Their minds refused to entertain it. Surely this couldn't be happening to them.

Nor did Phyllis need to be told a second time to "hold on to his wee hand."

She did. And she would. For as long as necessary.

Until "It" happened.

They didn't have long to wait. Sister Brush had been right.

The darkness of night was beginning to obscure the foggy grey of the foggy day. Street lamps were struggling to stretch piercing fingers of light into the encircling fog.

It was ten to five.

Thomas give a tiny smile.

Then a heavy sigh.

And departed for heaven.

There was an uncanny eerie silence.

The laboured breathing had ceased.

The beeping of the monitor had stopped.

So this was death.

This was the final parting. The last instalment. The ultimate repayment.

This was "It".

Suddenly the silence was broken by a shrill scream.

"Thomas! Thomas! My wee Thomas!"

It was Phyllis. A mother's piercing wail.

She took her "wee Thomas" in her arms. And held on to him.

Hertford and she felt that they just wanted to run away again, taking their little treasure with them. Hide him away somewhere.

For them to see. To visit. To hold. Forever.

After allowing the absolutely beside-themselves parents a lengthy period of uninterrupted deeply personal grief, Sister Brush appeared again.

When she had sympathised feelingly with Hertford and Phyllis, she guided them towards reality again.

It was difficult. Oh so difficult! Almost impossible.

"Would you like to have him home later on tonight?" she enquired, sensitively.

"Yes, we would. Of course we would."

These were the understandable words of a grief-stricken mother whose mind was struggling through the fog of a mythical world of disbelief.

Of course, what else would they want?

Of course they wanted their Thomas home.

"Well then, I'm really awfully sorry but I will have to take him away now. Some preparations have to be made you know," she explained, with infinite tenderness.

"We know that. We know," said Hertford.

"Go ahead."

Those last two words didn't come easily. They took some strength to say.

Phyllis couldn't say anything now. She was speechless. Struck dumb.

Hertford and Phyllis stood, side by side, numb with grief and stunned with shock, watching their Thomas, covered with a sheet, being wheeled away from them, out of the ward and down the corridor.

Tears flowed freely from swollen reddened eyes.

How could they be expected, ever, ever, ever to understand THIS?

CHAPTER NINETEEN

'Safe In The Arms Of Jesus'

✤✤✤

Hertford and Phyllis drove home from the Hospital in absolute silence. They were dazed. Confused. Dumbfounded.

As they approached their bungalow, down the lane, they noticed that all the curtains had been drawn. Caring relatives had been there before them. To help prepare them for what lay ahead. The sense of loss. The tragedy of bereavement.

Moving towards the front door, the heart-broken parents were able to see up the hall through the glass panel.

Wendsley was lying in the hall, rolling over. They hesitated weeping, on the step. How were they going to tell him that his big brother, his playmate, wouldn't be coming back any more? How could they get him to understand that he would never become excited again at the sound of the big loud bleeper on the big yellow bus, for it wouldn't be coming back?

When they had composed themselves sufficiently, Hertford and Phyllis stepped inside their home. Although a number of kind and loving relatives were there, waiting to comfort them, they were struck immediately by an impression of emptiness. There was a feeling that something, someone, some vital part, was missing. And was gone for good.

Things were never going to be the same again.

Unable for the moment to face all the assembled well-wishers, Phyllis scooped Wendsley up from the floor, and carried him into her bedroom. There she sat with him on her knee, and cried and cried.

How could she ever attempt to explain all this to him? How could she explain how she felt to anybody? It would be impossible.

It brought some sense of comfort to have Wendsley on her knee. Hugging him tightly. At least he was still there.

At a quarter-to-nine the undertaker arrived. With a little coffin.

Phyllis stayed well out of the way while Hertford and some others removed Wendsley's cot from the boys' bedroom, so that Thomas could be left in his own room.

When all the minor removals had been completed, Phyllis entered the room.

Thomas was home. That was what she had wanted.

As she sat, alone and grief stricken, in that room with the body of her little son, Phyllis realised something else.

Something different. Something comforting.

As she looked at the wallpaper which she and Hertford had chosen for their sons' bedroom back in those happy moving-in decorating days, she remembered something which she had often said.

"I love the way the clouds and the rainbows are looking down on the boys," she had remarked. "This is their own little heaven."

There dawned upon her numbed soul the consciousness of a tremendous and indisputable fact.

Thomas was now IN heaven. The real heaven. The heaven of heavens. Where God lives.

He was looking down on the clouds and rainbows! And on her, sitting there alone, distracted by grief.

Thomas was now at home. In his final, eternal, happy home.

Her ever-so-slightly-soothing reverie was interrupted by Hertford entering the room.

"Phyllis, the undertaker would like to speak to us for a few minutes. Some things he needs to know about what we want put into the paper. Can you face it?" he enquired.

"Oh yes. Don't worry Hertford. I will come," she replied, and followed her husband into the living-room.

Wendsley lay on the floor, gazing up at the three adults, towering above him, as they began to talk.

"There are just some details which I need to know so that I can put a notice in the paper," the undertaker explained.

Hertford and Phyllis nodded. They were going to find it tough. But they understood. The man had his job to do.

"There are three main items," he went on. "Firstly, what was his full name? Then what age was he? And finally, what time do you want the funeral at? I presume you will want it on Thursday."

Hertford took responsibility for answering the questions. Supplying the information.

"He was Thomas Jackson Arnold. He was six years of age. Well, five years and ten months to be exact. And I suppose one o'clock would be a suitable time to have the funeral at, if that suits you."

As he noted down the details which he had been given, and confirmed the time of the funeral on Thursday 16th November, the undertaker was conscious of something tugging on his trouser leg.

He looked down.

It was Wendsley, with a tiny handful of trouser leg, holding on tightly.

"What an attractive little boy," he remarked. "He has such a charming smile. And what lovely red hair!"

This observation, made ever so kindly, jolted Phyllis. Took her right back to the night of his birth. Wasn't that what the nurse had said? All she had said.

"Believe it or not, Bertie," Hertford disclosed, "but Wendsley is handicapped as well."

"Oh is he? I didn't realise." The undertaker was obviously surprised.

He could be forgiven for not realising. No one did, unless told, for Wendsley just looked like any other little boy.

Phyllis by now had found her voice. Regained sufficient composure to allow her to contribute to the conversation.

"Wendsley is really going to miss Thomas," she reflected. "They were great playmates. Spent hours together, just rolling over and over on the floor. He won't know what has happened to him."

Acutely aware of the fact that Phyllis was in a very unstable emotional state, the undertake prepared to leave.

"I must go now and see to these things," he said, moving towards the door. Then turning as though he had suddenly remembered something which he should never have forgotten, he asked, "Oh by the way, is there anything else you want me to add to the notice for the paper? I mean like a verse from the Bible or anything like that."

The question didn't apply to Hertford. He didn't know any verses from the Bible.

Phyllis was the one who knew. She hadn't thought of a suitable verse from the Bible, but there was one title of a hymn that she thought she would like.

"Could you just put in 'Safe in the arms of Jesus'?" she requested.

"No problem," was the immediate response. "That sounds like a most appropriate line."

Phyllis thought so too.

She was sure that Thomas was there. It described precisely the position as it had been revealed to her, in silent meditation.

In heaven. "Safe in the arms of Jesus".

Relatives began to arrive. In twos and threes they came. Sombrely dressed, and full of sympathy for Hertford and Phyllis. They hugged the young couple warmly and expressed their condolences so sincerely.

"We are very sorry for what has happened," they whispered. "Awfully sorry. Don't be a bit afraid to let us know if there is anything at all we can do."

There was genuine heart felt grief.

A real sense of death. The death of a child.

Phyllis was so distressed that she felt she wasn't thinking straight. She didn't know her own mind.

It was this mystical sense of the unreal, again.

When was she going to waken up out of this? Was it not just a bad dream? A nightmare?

When was she going to come to her senses?

As midnight approached, a local doctor arrived to see Phyllis, who was by that time lying on the bed. She was staring at the ceiling, too drained, too exhausted, even to cry. In a stupor of grief.

"I'm really sorry about Thomas," the doctor began, with deep feeling.

After waiting a moment she went on, "And how are you coping, Mrs Arnold? Do you want any tablets to calm you down?"

"No. I don't need anything I'm sure," Phyllis replied. "I think I will be O.K. But I am a bit worried about Wendsley. He seems to be taking another cold."

"Don't worry about Wendsley," the doctor was reassuring. "I will listen to his chest and get him an antibiotic which will probably clear it up in a few days."

When she had invited Phyllis to ring her "at any time" if she needed anything, the doctor left the room.

She found Wendsley in the living room with his dad and some others.

Having given him a thorough examination she then returned to the bedroom, to Phyllis.

She had just had an idea. A good, sensible idea.

"Mrs Arnold, I have just sounded Wendsley's chest. He has a slight infection, but nothing to worry about. However, I could have him admitted to Craigavon Hospital, at least until after the funeral.

If you would be agreeable to that, then Wendsley could be given any treatment he needs, and you could rest assured that he was being well cared for," she suggested.

Phyllis agreed that this would be a satisfactory solution. Ford was already being cared for by helpful relatives. Now Wendsley would be well looked after also. It was a prudent plan.

The doctor phoned the Hospital there and then and made all the necessary arrangements.

Thus it was, that in the early hours of the morning, on Wednesday 15th November, Hertford and his brother-in-law Estlin took Wendsley into Craigavon Hospital.

He was wheeled into the same ward out of which Thomas had been wheeled some seven hours before.

Hertford and Estlin drove home from the Hospital in absolute silence.

Minds were numb. Speech was frozen.

Visibility was down to eight to ten yards.

The fog was terrible.

It hadn't lifted.

CHAPTER TWENTY

Stairway To Heaven

✤ ✤ ✤

It was the morning of the funeral. Thursday 16th November. Silent preparations were being made in the hushed house.

Hertford and his brother Tyrrell were standing at the back door, having a smoke. They stood on the ramp, backs against the wall. In absolute silence they lit one cigarette after another.

As they stood there, chilled and damp, but glad, nonetheless, to be outside, something happened before their eyes. Something which hadn't happened for weeks.

The fog began to lift.

Big shafts of sunlight broke through the clouds. They lit up patches of stubble on the field behind the house. Suddenly, for the first time for ages, something had pierced the gloom. A patchwork of light was woven on the field.

The two brothers stood beholding.

"Wouldn't you just think those shafts of sunlight were big ladders coming down to take Thomas away? Away up to heaven," Hertford remarked at length.

That was the whole conversation. All that was said. Hertford and Tyrrell didn't say any more. They just remained, silently weeping. Each engrossed in his own thoughts.

When they did eventually re-enter the house, Tyrrell re-joined the others who were flitting from the lounge to the kitchen and back. Wanting to do something but not knowing what to do. Wanting to say something, but not knowing what to day.

Hertford went into the bedroom where Phyllis was.

She was sitting alone. It was where she wanted to be.

She couldn't bear to see people.

She didn't want to hear people, no matter how kind and caring they were. She had got beyond that.

All she wanted was to be alone. Solitude.

"At least that old fog is away," Hertford said. "It's getting really clear outside."

Phyllis nodded. She couldn't think of anything to say.

It was probably good that the fog was away, but it felt as though she hadn't seen or been outside for days.

The clock seemed to race along that morning. With the flurry of people coming and going, awaiting the funeral, the morning soon passed.

Much tea was made. Some of it was drunk.

At twelve-fifty the big black hearse drew up at the door. There was a heavy monotonous drone off it.

One o'clock came

The weather had cleared. There was a cloudless sky. The first time for many days.

The crowd was unbelievable. The whole countryside had turned out. People spilled out of the bungalow at the front and at the back.

The drive was lined. The lane was lined.

Some walked behind the hearse. Some stood and watched, for the lane was so thick with people that there wasn't anywhere for them to walk.

Many wept.

The funeral procession walked the mile between the bungalow and the village of Donacloney.

There was a simple church service, and then it was off to the cemetery in Dromore.

As they drove along, the sun was winter-low in the sky and the shadow of the hearse could be seen moving along in the hedgerows which had changed from summer green through autumn gold to winter bleak.

It was sunset when they left Dromore to come home. Four-thirty. The sun was setting in a ball of fire.

When Hertford and Phyllis arrived back at the bungalow there were people everywhere. Seemed like there had been an invasion. They only stayed half-an-hour.

"Let's go to the Hospital and see Wendsley," suggested Phyllis.

"Good idea," agreed Hertford, who was so restless that he didn't know what to do, "Come on."

With that they went out into the car and set off.

As they were driving between Lurgan and Portadown, roundabout after roundabout, Phyllis looked over at Hertford. He was lighting up yet another cigarette.

Suddenly she shouted, "Stop the car! Stop the car!"

Hertford was startled, "What's wrong Phyllis? What's wrong?" he enquired anxiously.

He didn't stop the car, but slowed down to deal with this sudden emergency which seemed to have arisen.

"It's us Hertford," she began to explain. "It's us. We are not ready to die. If anything happens to you or me we will never see Thomas again. Thomas is in heaven. What has been the point of it all if we are never going to see him again?"

He didn't like to admit it openly, but Hertford had been thinking the very same thing.

"I tell you what we will do," he determined. "Hold on until we see Wendsley. Then when we get home we will have somebody round to sort this all out."

Phyllis was satisfied with that.

Things certainly all needed to be "sorted out".

When they arrived in the Hospital ward, Wendsley was pulling himself up on the bars of his cot.

This was something new. Something encouraging. Another shaft of sunlight, to pierce the surrounding gloom.

His despondent parents had never witnessed him make such a sustained effort to pull himself up before.

A doctor joined them in the ward.

"Wendsley is ready for home any time," he told them. "But we will keep him here for a few more days to allow you both to settle down after what you have been through. Would you like that?"

"That would be marvellous," Phyllis agreed.

As he was leaving the ward the doctor said, "Just give us a few hours notice and you can have him home."

When the three of them were left together again in the ward, Phyllis and Hertford sat on either side of Wendsley's cot. Watching him. Helping him. Trying bravely to smile at him.

After a short time Phyllis put her head down on her hand and cried in misery.

"Lord, is this why you gave us two handicapped boys?" she asked aloud, in anguish. "So that you could take the one and leave the other?"

There seemed to be so many questions.

So few answers.

CHAPTER TWENTY-ONE

The Dream Of Death

✤ ✤ ✤

Later on that Thursday evening Hertford and Phyllis arrived home. Things were quieter. The crowds had dispersed.

Finally, the last of the close relations bade their tearful farewells. The grieving parents were left alone.

They decided to go to bed early. They were physically exhausted, mentally numb and emotionally upset.

Rest was a top priority.

Eventually, in the small hours of Friday morning, they cried themselves to sleep.

Their sleep, however, was not the contented sleep of a tired body. It was the restless sleep of a tormented mind.

It was in the middle of that night, while in a troubled state of soul, that Hertford had a dream.

He saw it all plainly. It was frighteningly real. He felt that he was reliving the most unpleasant experience of his life all over again. Moment by moment. Dust to dust. Tear by tear.

In his dream Hertford was back in the cemetery in Dromore. He saw the crowds and felt the chill of the November day.

It was strange the way in which the end-of-the-day sun lit up the faces of the mourners, around the open grave. They all had a pale orange glow.

Looking into the grave, he saw the nameplate on the coffin. Thomas Jackson Arnold.

Then came the clods of earth. Clattering and thumping dully on to the little coffin.

Gradually, slowly, it was covered …

In this horrible realistic dream there was a message for him. He felt it. He knew it. He was terrified by it.

The message was simple, and it was clear as day.

Death was coming back.

Hertford awoke. Petrified.

He reached over in the bed and shook Phyllis awake.

"Wake up! Wake up Phyllis!" he urged.

"What's wrong with you Hertford?" she asked, startled to have been so suddenly awakened. Here they were, having their first chance to get a really good sleep for ages, and Hertford was waking her up in the middle of the night.

He switched on the bedside lamp.

Covering her eyes from the instant glare, Phyllis looked over at him.

She was shocked by what she saw.

Her husband was as white as a sheet. Sweat was sitting in beads on his forehead and running down his temples.

When he saw her looking over, Hertford said tersely, "Come on, Phyllis we will have to get up. Get up there! Quickly!"

"What on earth has got into you Hertford?" Phyllis enquired, more sympathetically. She could see that he was trembling. She also remembered that less than twelve hours before she had shouted at him to stop the car.

"Death is coming back, Phyllis," Hertford said, obviously frightened. "I know it. I've just had a terrible dream. I saw the funeral, the grave, the coffin, and it's coming back again. The dream made it plain."

"Calm down there, Hertford," his wife advised. She was wide awake now, and realised that she would have to settle her husband somehow.

"Don't worry about death now, Hertford," she soothed.

"Thomas is in heaven, and the doctor says that Wendsley is going to be O.K. We can bring him home any time we want."

"You don't understand what I am trying to tell you, Phyllis," her husband replied, frustrated. He was almost frantic by now.

"Death is coming back. But it's not Wendsley that I am worried about. It's ME. Death is coming back for ME and I'm not ready!"

Hertford had taken to pacing anxiously up and down the bedroom floor. Phyllis sat on the edge of the bed. Sleeping was probably finished for the night.

"I am going to have to do something about this!" Hertford was almost shouting now in his frenzy. "I am going to have to talk to somebody. There must be somebody, somewhere, who can tell me how to get right with God.

I must make my peace with God, before I die.

For death is coming back!

And it's coming for ME!"

CHAPTER TWENTY-TWO

Saved!

✤✤✤

What remained of that night was spent in earnest discussion.

"Who do I know who could tell me what to do? How do I get ready to go to heaven when I die, for death is coming for me? And how can I be sure about it?"

These were the questions that Hertford asked repeatedly. Often audibly, occasionally inwardly.

Finally, after much anguished thought and consideration, the answer came. When it did, Hertford was convinced that it was the right one.

There was somebody whom he knew who would be able to tell him all he needed to find out so urgently.

It was somebody who had made a lasting impression on him as a boy in Secondary School. It was a man for whom he had the greatest respect.

It was Tom Somerville.

Tom had been his Religious Education teacher some sixteen years earlier. He had also visited Thomas when he was in Hospital. Hertford always recognised that there was something different about Tom. He always seemed to have a deep sense of quiet confidence and inner peace.

He was in touch with God.

When he had waited until breakfast time, Hertford could wait no longer. To him, at that moment, getting ready for heaven was the pressing priority.

He rang Tom.

Hertford wondered if his former teacher would resent him calling so early in the morning.

"I'm glad to hear you, Hertford. Would be glad to hear you at any time," was the reassuring reply. "What can I do for you?"

"Well, it's just like this, Tom ..." Hertford began, then poured out his heart to an understanding and sympathetic listener.

He reminded Tom of Thomas's illness and death. He retold, in all its vivid detail, the dream of the night before, and explained how he felt that death was now on his track. And was closing in on him fast.

"Hertford, it is quite obvious to me what is happening here. God is trying to speak to you. When can we meet and talk about all this?" Tom replied.

In the course of his explanations Hertford had mentioned the fact that Wendsley was in Craigavon Hospital.

They arranged to meet in the Hospital at eleven-thirty that morning.

True to his word, Tom Somerville arrived into the ward to Hertford, Phyllis and little Wendsley at eleven-thirty. He spoke to the parents graciously, sympathising with them about the death of Thomas. Acutely aware, however, that a busy hospital ward in the middle of a busy morning would not be the most suitable place to hold a conversation about the weighty matters that were on all of their minds, Tom invited Hertford and Phyllis to come home with him.

"Could you spare a few minutes from Wendsley to come round to my house for a cup of tea and a chat?" he asked.

The invitation was readily accepted.

Here was Hertford's opportunity to do what he had promised twice in the previous twenty-four hours, that he must do soon. Talk to somebody. Get all these things sorted out!

They were only in the house a short time when Tom said, "You know, Hertford, Thomas is in heaven."

"I don't need anybody to tell me that, Tom. Where else could he be?" was Hertford's immediate response.

"Well you know then, if you ever want to see him again, you will have to be saved."

Tom was pursuing the subject.

The anxious, frustrated soul was equally emphatic in his response to Tom's second statement.

"Tom, I know that as well," he said. "I know that I need something. I'm quite sure that I'm not ready for heaven.

"You could get saved here today. Right now, you know," Tom went on.

"Oh, I didn't realise it could be as simple or as quick as that, Tom," the former pupil replied.

"I thought you had to go to church for a long time. And pay in a pile of money. I thought that maybe playing the organ or singing in the choir would help too. Does it not take years before you can really say that you are a Christian?"

This instant salvation, this "saved right now" idea, was obviously a new one on Hertford.

"Salvation is a gift, not a reward," Tom explained, "You need to realise that you are a sinner and need God. You can acknowledge that Jesus died on Calvary to take away your sins, and ask Him into your heart. And you can do it at this very moment."

This was what Hertford wanted. What he was craving for. His sins taken away. Above all, what he most desired, was the assurance that he would be in heaven, with Thomas, when death arrived to take him.

There and then Hertford fell to his knees at a chair. Pouring out an agonised soul in stumbling speech, he repented of his sins and asked the Lord Jesus Christ to come into his heart.

To cleanse him.

To fit him for heaven.

When Hertford had finished he remained kneeling. Face buried in the cushions. Tom rose slowly, reverently, happily, from where he had been kneeling beside his former pupil. It was a great encouragement to him to hear the outpouring of a penitent soul coming to the Saviour.

It was fruit for his labour. An answer to his prayers.

As Hertford began to rise from his kneeling position, Tom exclaimed, "Praise the Lord, Hertford you are saved!"

It couldn't have been that straightforward surely. Hertford was convinced that he missed something somewhere.

"Hold on there a minute, Tom" he cautioned. "This must all be a load of nonsense. I have heard nothing. Seen nothing. Felt nothing. How could I possibly be saved? I don't feel one bit different."

Tom smiled.

He was so wise. So experienced. So patient.

"You are not saved by your feelings. Hertford," he counselled. "You are saved by your faith. It is an open heart operation."

Hertford thought about this for a minute or two.

It was interesting. At odds with all his preconceived ideas. All new stuff to him.

Then he had another thought. It was related to something which he had learnt many years before.

One of his earlier brushes with religion had been in school, where he had been taught the Lord's Prayer. In it, he seemed to remember, there was a bit about, "forgive us our trespasses as we forgive those who trespass against us."

He voiced his concern.

"Tom, if I'm supposed to be a Christian now," he asked sincerely, "does that mean that I should forgive everybody who has done anything against me? Mind you I feel pretty bitter about some of the things that have happened in my life."

"Are you going to let things that happened, possibly years ago, spoil your experience of peace with God, your assurance of a home in heaven?" Tom answered one question by asking another.

Hertford realised that he wasn't going to let anything spoil his peace with God, or do him out of his place in heaven.

As he pondered it, the incidents which had galled him for so long seemed to pale into insignificance. The hurts seemed to be miraculously healed.

Then came the marvellous, glorious revelation.

He was different after all. He had been saved. He was changed!

As the lively conversation about things like "new birth" and "the importance of regular prayer times" continued, a fresh desire for an old habit flooded back to Hertford.

His body seemed to crave it.

Something unexplained within him seemed to resist it.

The craving conquered.

"I'm sorry, Tom," Hertford confessed, ashamedly, "but I am going to have to out outside for a smoke."

"Not at all, Hertford, You don't need to go outside. Sure you can have your smoke in here," Tom replied.

As he drew the cigarette packet from his pocket, the new convert looked like a guilty schoolboy.

He was changed though, wasn't he? ...

"I suppose you are going to tell me that I will have to quit these," he remarked.

"I didn't tell you to quit anything" came the reply. "It will come to you. God will take away the desire."

And He did.

Hertford had a smoke that day. He felt he needed it. Gradually, though, the desire to smoke disappeared, just as Tom had predicted. He went from smoking forty a day to none a day in a fortnight. And he hasn't smoked since.

Such was the mighty transformation that God worked in his life.

He definitely WAS a changed man.

As Hertford, now growing in confidence in his new-found faith, and a mixed-up, but happy-for-Hertford, Phyllis, prepared to leave, Tom restrained them.

"Wait there a wee minute," he said, "I have something which I would like to give each of you."

With that he left the room and returned very shortly with a red Gideon New Testament each for Hertford and Phyllis.

He had even take the trouble to write their names on them.

"I have underlined a verse in your little New Testaments," he said. "And I have put a marker at the place so that you can find it easily."

When Hertford and Phyllis turned to the marked verse in their newly acquired New Testaments, this is what they read:-

"For He has rescued us from the dominion of darkness and brought us into the kingdom of the Son He loves, in whom we have redemption, the forgiveness of sins." (Colossians 1. v 13 N.I.V.)

When he read this, Hertford could scarcely believe it.

Could this possibly be true? Did it actually refer to him? Was he somewhere in the "we" and "us" of the verse?

Could it be that Hertford Arnold, the scoffer and the sceptic, was now a child of God, a citizen of the kingdom of God, redeemed and forgiven?

There was more blessing to this being saved than he had ever imagined.

He was sure now that he was saved.

He was delighted about that.

He was sure as well that he was going to be in heaven with Christ, and Thomas, when he died.

He was delighted about that too.

CHAPTER TWENTY-THREE

'The Wise Shepherd'

✤ ✤ ✤

Immediately after leaving Tom's house, Hertford and Phyllis returned to Craigavon Hospital. Although Hertford was now rejoicing in his new found faith, and Phyllis was happy for him, their hospital days weren't over.

Wendsley was still there, and they wanted to be with him. To help him, to comfort him, to be company for him, as much as they could.

During the afternoon the doctor came into the ward. "Wendsley is doing well," he informed them. "He is ready for home any time."

The parents considered this proposition carefully.

Though Wendsley was probably ready for home, they decided that perhaps they weren't ready to have him back so soon.

They were both still physically and emotionally drained after the experiences of the previous week. Besides that, the weather was still very cold and foggy. Not ideal conditions for a sick child with a weak chest to be outside. Wendsley was going to be with them for a long time to come, so they reckoned that it would be better to postpone bringing him home for another day or two. He would then be fully recovered and they would be in better spirits to receive him.

They told the doctor what they had decided, and he understood.

Everyone agreed that Sunday would be a suitable day to have Wendsley home, and this was arranged.

However, when Hertford and Phyllis arrived at the Hospital on the Sunday morning to collect their little son, how things had changed! Drastically, and for the worse.

As they entered the ward a doctor met them. He looked glum.

"I'm sorry," he said, "but I'm afraid Wendsley won't be able to get home today. He has picked up some kind of virus and has been very sick during the night. This morning he will not eat a thing for us here. We just wouldn't be happy to allow him home, at least for another day or two."

The parents were shocked. They thought that with all they had passed through they would be beyond being stunned. They weren't.

Again came this incredible feeling of disbelief.

"But he was all right last night when we left," Phyllis replied. She was struggling to take it in. "He was smiling and playing like he always did."

"I know that Mrs Arnold," the doctor continued, sympathetically. "This has happened so suddenly that it has taken everyone in here by surprise."

His countenance matched the conversation. He looked startled, too.

Hertford and Phyllis spend Sunday and Monday in the Hospital. It was distressing to watch the deterioration in Wendsley's condition.

On Tuesday morning his breathing became laboured. He was wheeled away to have a chest x-ray. In the afternoon it was time for the results.

The parents met the doctor in a side-room of the main ward. It all seemed so horribly familiar. What would the result of the x-ray be?

"The x-rays show that both of Wendsley's lungs are clouded over white," the doctor said. "He would appear to have viral pneumonia in both lungs."

There was that dreaded word again.

A stunned silence followed the doctor's statement.

There was a sense of having seen it all before. Of being able to predict almost the next development. Possibly even the next word.

Hertford and Phyllis didn't speak. They couldn't. Speechless yet again.

The doctor broke the awkward hush. It was a different doctor, different room, different set of x-ray plates, and yet what he had to say was almost exactly the same as they had heard about Thomas less than two weeks before.

"Wendsley has just deteriorated so fast that we couldn't believe it," he told them. "Every time I go out of the ward and return maybe half-an-hour later and he has gone downhill even more. We will continue to do all in our power to keep him here. But really he is now in the hands of God."

Again it was so familiar.

Beyond the touch of tender loving care.

Beyond the scope of medical science.

Into the hands of God.

Throughout that Tuesday night the hospital vigil continued. Doctors and nurses moved silently to and fro in the ward, checking the monitors, adjusting the drips.

Mid-morning on Wednesday and Wendsley had lapsed into a semi-conscious state.

Phyllis craved seclusion. Solitude. Isolation.

She felt she had to close herself away from the goings-on in the ward.

So, leaving Hertford sitting with Wendsley, she fell to her knees beside the settee in the little room reserved for the relatives of patients. She had spent many hours of heart-searching misery in that room over the previous few days.

Now she was in total desperation.

"Lord, You couldn't take Wendsley on us too. This just can't be real!"

She was pouring out her pent-up emotions to God, again.

"Lord, heal him! Please!

Get him better!

Don't let him die!

Don't let him die!

Please, Lord, please!"

Rising from that settee, on to legs shaky from sleepless nights and stressful days, a strange realisation enfolded her.

She knew in her breaking heart that God was in control.

Somewhat calmed in her soul, but still dreading the coming hours, perhaps days, Phyllis rejoined Hertford at Wendsley's bedside.

Shortly after three o'clock that afternoon, the ward door slid quietly open.

It was Norrie Emerson, a friend, to see them.

"I was working in the yard there after dinner-time" the visitor said, "and I just couldn't get you out of my mind. I had been praying for you both all morning, and I felt compelled to come and see you. I hope you don't mind."

"We don't mind at all," Phyllis replied, "It is very kind of you to take off your work to come and see us."

Norrie's care and concern for the crushed couple was demonstrated in his next action.

Opening up his jacket he produced from an inside pocket, a piece of folded paper. "I have a poem here for you," he said. "Read it over a few times when I leave. It will help you both to see a meaning in all of this I'm sure."

When he reached forward and handed the poem to Phyllis her heart skipped a beat. She was conscious of a shake in her outstretched hand.

Another poem! A third one.

The previous two poems had been given to her, one before, one after, tragic events in her life.

Could this be an omen. A sign of things to come?

Sensing that Phyllis was probably scared, but certainly, at least, uneasy, Norrie enquired, "Do you mind if I pray with the three of you before I leave?"

"Not at all, please do," Hertford responded immediately. He had a high regard for the out-and-out sincerity of a busy man who would leave his work in the middle of the afternoon to come and try to comfort them. In addition to that, he had also learned over the few turbulent days since his conversion, the vital importance of prayer in the Christian life.

When he had prayed with deep feeling, Norrie put his arms around both Hertford and Phyllis.

They were all weeping.

Then noiselessly, almost reverently, as he had come, he slipped from the ward, leaving the heartbroken parents and their very sick son to each other and to God.

Phyllis unfolded the piece of paper. Her husband watched her from across the cot.

Blinking away the tears, she read the poem:-

The Wise Shepherd

The Story is told of a shepherd wise
Who when the day was done
Needed to cross a stream to get home
He led but the sheep wouldn't come.

So he gently turned to the flock once more
Knowing that this was the best
He stopped and lifted the tiniest lamb
Holding it safe on his breast.

While he waded the troublesome stream again
In the light of the setting sun.
This time there was no hesitation at all
For they followed him every one.

Oh I wonder if Christ our Shepherd Divine
Doesn't work in the selfsame way.
By taking the dear little lambs to draw
The sheep that have gone astray.

Oftentimes He has tried, yes so very long
To get us to follow His call
And when everything fails, He takes to Himself
The tiniest lamb of all.

To punish us? No! He loves us so much
That He died for our sins to atone.
But He hopes when the lambs are all safe in the fold,
That the sheep will follow Him home.

After she had read it a few times she handed it across the cot where her "tiny lamb" was battling for life to Hertford, who was devastated also.

He read it in silence, making no attempt to comment.

Phyllis reclaimed the poem and read it yet again.

God was really speaking to her. Convicting her.

So this was the message.

God, in His infinite wisdom, had removed one of her lambs into His fold of joy and peace and freedom from pain, and He was now in the process of carrying the second one home as well.

Could she, would she, follow?

Although she had been saved years before in Moira, she had lost her joy, her peace, her sense of direction. She was going round in spiritual circles. That was when she went anywhere at all.

Her Shepherd had called her and she had followed Him gladly once. Now He was asking her to rise up and follow Him again. The Shepherd was taking her lambs, and it was He who was leading her home.

The first line of the last verse was a comfort to her, though. It dispelled a long-held belief, a sneaking fear.

She had often been convinced that God was punishing her for her lack of commitment, and for her backslidden life.

It wasn't so.

God wasn't punishing her. He was tenderly calling her.

What a tremendous difference!

That evening Phyllis was frightened. Hurt. Scared.

Wendsley's condition was deteriorating rapidly.

Hour by hour. It seemed even minute by minute.

She knew in her heart that he was going to die.

Nothing could prevent it now.

CHAPTER TWENTY-FOUR

'My Wee Soldier'

❖ ❖ ❖

Not only was Wendsley's condition so distressing for his distraught parents, but it also affected the whole wider family circle as well.

They just couldn't believe it!

A steady soundless stream of relatives poured into the ward all that Wednesday night and early Thursday morning. They stood struck dumb, helpless with grief, watching the medical staff as they nursed little Wendsley, attending to his every need.

An ominous silence settled on the ward. It was like the muffling, smothering, all-pervasive fog outside.

Hertford and Phyllis were totally shattered.

They were numbed by the sense of absolute helplessness.

If only they could do something miraculous. Or buy something marvellous. Or contact some mighty healer.

But they couldn't. They were powerless to alter the situation. They couldn't for one second stay the ebbing tide of their little one's life.

How true it was what the doctor had said.

Wendsley was now in the hands of God.

They had to leave him there.

The only things they could do were the small and tender things. Like wiping his brow, combing his hair, holding his hand, straightening his bedclothes.

These they did over and over again.

Four o'clock came and Phyllis was almost at breaking point. She left the ward to go back to seek solitude in the relative's room. Her mother came in to comfort her a number of times.

After about forty minutes Hertford joined her in the little room. He was beside himself too.

He put his arms around his weeping wife.

"I think you had better come in here now, Phyllis." he said, through the tears. "The doctor says his pulse is getting very shallow. It won't be long now. Come with me, and we will both go in together."

With that Hertford took Phyllis's shaking hand in his strong one, and they returned to the hush of the ward.

It was almost four-forty five, nine days to the minute from their eldest son had died, when the parents approached their youngest son's bed, hand in hand.

Suddenly Wendsley gave a short sigh.

Then there was stillness.

There was a monotonous hum from the heart monitor. The line was straight. The heartbeat had ceased.

Wendsley had passed away.

Simultaneously, Hertford and Phyllis both screeched, "Wendsley! Wendsley!"

Hertford lifted the body of his little son into a sitting position in the bed.

"My wee soldier!

My wee man!

Mummy and daddy love you!

Oh, my wee man! My wee soldier."

In his anguish he repeated these words, time and time again.

The doctor came forward and removed the drips so that both parents could spend some precious final minutes with the frail earthly body in which their beloved Wendsley had once dwelt.

The ward filled up with sobbing, silent relatives

The only sounds were the sounds of grief.

Some open public weeping, some more muted.
A succession of sighs and the rustle of paper handkerchiefs.
Wendsley and Thomas were together again.
Safe in the arms of Jesus.
On the shoulders of the Shepherd.
Marvellous for them. What a relief!
Tragic for Hertford and Phyllis. What a catastrophe!
Losing two children in less than two weeks.
How could they ever cope with THIS?

CHAPTER TWENTY-FIVE

'Yes, Jesus Loves Me'

✤ ✤ ✤

The bewildered parents drove home in almost total silence. The only sound to be heard above the noise of the engine were deep heavy sighs and the occasional vigorous blowing of the nose.

There was little they could say.

As they sped along Phyllis found that a verse of the poem which had been given to her on the previous afternoon, kept repeating itself in her mind. She couldn't seem to escape it.

"Oftentimes He has tried, yes, so very long

To get us to follow His call ..."

These words struck like a dagger into her heart. They were so true. Her whole thought pattern became dominated by these words, ringing in her brain.

Even the fuss back at the Hospital was out of her mind now.

Something dramatic was happening.

God was speaking directly to her.

Hertford was saved now. That was a blessing. She was glad about that. She had prayed for him so earnestly when she was younger.

Now the tables were turned. She was now the one in the throes of spiritual conviction.

She too had been saved, that night in Moira twelve years before. But she had lost interest in the things of God. Turned her back on Him.

God was now graciously calling her again.

"And when everything fails, He takes to Himself
The tiniest lamb of all."

Phyllis was heartbroken that it had to come to this. God wanted her back to Him so badly that He had taken to Himself her youngest child, her "tiniest lamb of all." Not to punish her as she had once imagined, but to lead her back to the fold.

They were both overwhelmed by grief when they drove up to the front of their bungalow.

Everything was so still.

There was an awesome, almost frightening hush.

No-one was around. Ford was being cared for by other relatives, and nobody else had arrived.

They were on their own.

Phyllis stood on the doorstep, weeping inconsolably.

Nine days before, when she had come home from Hospital, grief stricken, and looked through the glass door and up the hall, Wendsley had been lying there, rolling over and over.

She had been devastated then. Wondering how to tell him about Thomas, his brother, playmate and friend.

Now the hall was empty except for the cold unsympathetic furniture standing around.

There was no sound.

No movement.

No life.

No Wendsley.

He had gone too.

Standing there shaking on the step, a voice seemed to say to her, "And what about you? Thomas is at home with Me. Wendsley has joined him, at home in heaven. What about you?

The lambs are both safe in the fold, Phyllis.

Are you gong to follow them?"

As the broken-hearted mother pushed the door open to enter the hall, her soul was drawn to God. She realised again that this wasn't punishment. This was love. Caring love, patient love, Divine love.

Her Heavenly Father so much yearned for her return, that He was drawing her gently to Him.

When she stepped into the empty hall of their echoey-empty bungalow, her legs left her.

Phyllis was physically weak, emotionally distressed and spiritually shattered.

Collapsing to her knees on the floor, she cried out in anguish. "I have had it Lord, I can't go another step until I am sure that I don't miss out on heaven."

Then came the tears of repentance, the deep remorse.

"Lord, I'm really sorry that Thomas and Wendsley had to give their lives to bring Hertford to You for salvation, and to bring me to my senses so that I would come back to You," she wailed.

Hertford had gone in past his wife by this time. He was in the kitchen, searching for something which he would never have opened a month before, a hymn book.

"Lord, please give me back the joy of my salvation. I know that You have never left me. But I have left You, let You down, made a mess of my life."

Still the pathetic figure in the hall was praying fervently.

"Lord, I cannot go on another minute without You. It is only You has brought me to this point. And it is only You can help me from here on in. I will need You every day, every hour, every single minute of my life until I see Thomas and Wendsley again.

Please, please, help me Lord."

As she struggled to her feet a sense of the presence of the Lord enfolded her. She knew that God had heard her plea.

He was answering already.

During her outpourings to God, Phyllis had noticed Hertford crossing from the kitchen into the living-room.

When she went into the room, she found her husband sitting on the rug in front of the fire. The firelight played on his face. A hymn book lay open before him.

Flopping down beside Hertford, she put her arms around him. He stretched out an arm and pulled her towards him.

Looking down at the open page of the hymn book, a hymn seemed to jump out of the page at Phyllis.

"Let's sing that," she suggested to Hertford, pointing to her chosen hymn.

"We will sing it for Thomas and Wendsley. For Ford and for us. How true it is."

With tears of deep sorrow, mingled with tears of genuine relief, they sat close together in the firelight and sang huskily.

"Jesus loves me, this I know,
For the Bible tells me so,
Little ones to Him belong,
They are weak but He is strong."

It proved to be a tremendous boost to Phyllis and was a marvellous tonic to both of them.

It gave them a definite sense of purpose, combined with a strange sense of peace.

They were united in grief.

They were united by human affection.

Now they were united in their desire to live for Christ and rejoice in His wonderful love.

No matter what could happen in the days ahead they could face the uncertainty of the future in the absolute certainty of the truth of the chorus.

"Yes, Jesus loves me,
Yes, Jesus loves me,
Yes, Jesus loves me,
The Bible tells me so."

CHAPTER TWENTY-SIX

Some Party in Heaven

✤✤✤

Their sacred singing session was soon to be interrupted.

Mourners started to arrive at the house. Hertford and Phyllis just couldn't seem to believe it. It was so unreal.

Here they were, nine days on from the shock of the death of Thomas, and they were seeing the same kind-hearted people coming to say the same tender-hearted things to sympathise with them on the death of Wendsley.

At nine o'clock the undertaker arrived with the little white coffin. He was overwhelmed.

"In all my years in this job," he told the grieving parents, "I have never had an experience like this before."

He was so genuinely upset that he just asked for Wendsley's full name and age. He thought that he could handle nearly every situation that his work could present.

Nine days before he had looked down to see Wendsley tugging at his trouser leg. Now he was compiling his death notice for the paper.

This one nearly beat him.

"He was Wendsley John Arnold and he was just three years and two months old," Hertford told him. "He was born on the 29th September 1986."

With that information quickly noted, the undertaker left, only to return two days later for the funeral.

Saturday, 25th November, began with the same choking fog that had merged day into night for weeks on end.

In mid-morning the fog lifted and the sun came out.

The mourners walked from the bungalow to the church in Donacloney, in the first sunshine they had seen for days.

The lane was lined with men waiting to join the funeral. Many of them stood in the same positions as they had done nine days before.

It was uncanny.

The whole day seemed to be an action replay of the day when Thomas was buried, just over a week previously.

There was one important difference though.

It was in the people.

Since that day, Hertford had been saved and Phyllis had been restored to the Lord.

What a change it made!

Now, as they followed Wendsley's little coffin to the church they realised what it was all about.

Thomas had gone. And he hadn't come back. That was in spite of his anxious parents' vain hope that one day he would just reappear somehow.

They knew, now, that Wendsley had gone too. This was for real. He wouldn't sit in his high chair or roll on the floor again, either.

Their profound sorrow and many tears of that second funeral day were accompanied by a deep sense of inner peace.

They knew that where Thomas was, Wendsley was, and that was where they were both going, too.

What a consolation.

As they sat together in the back of the funeral car on the way home from the cemetery in Dromore, dusk was falling.

The sky was swallowing up the red ball of a sun. Everywhere seemed to be momentarily aflame.

The heavens were declaring the glory of God.

It seemed as though God was putting His seal to the end of a chapter in their lives.

The parents held hands.

They were acutely aware of the presence of God, the Mighty Creator, their Saviour.

Phyllis looked over at Hertford, tears glinting golden on her cheeks in the afterglow from the sunset sky.

"There must be some party in heaven right now," she remarked.

CHAPTER TWENTY-SEVEN

Black Christmas

✤ ✤ ✤

After the funerals came the darkest days of the winter.

Ford had been at home from school for a week. Then he went back.

Hertford had arranged for his father and brothers to look after the chicken house for him for a few days. Then he went back to his work down the yard.

With her husband and son out of the house Phyllis decided to do some cleaning. It would keep her mind occupied.

As she worked her way along the hall with the vacuum cleaner she stopped at the door of the boys' bedroom and looked in.

The teddy bears and toys were still there. They stood, sat and lay respectfully around, as though awaiting the return of their owners.

The room was spic and span. Clean and tidy.

And empty.

Phyllis switched off the cleaner.

She felt so guilty.

Thomas had gone. Never to come back.

Wendsley had gone. Never to come back.

And yet everything in the household returned to normal.

Ford had gone back to school. Hertford was down in the chicken house again, and she was cleaning the house as she had always done.

Phyllis stood in the hall and prayed.

"Lord, if You are really here, please reveal Yourself to me."

Too unsettled to continue with the vacuuming she went into the kitchen and sat down at the end of the table.

She felt ashamed with herself, lonely and all mixed up.

Reaching up to a nearby shelf she lifted down her Bible. She had never been in the habit of looking for verses at random, but on this particular occasion she felt that it was the thing to do.

Flicking slowly through her Bible she prayed silently, "Lord, please give me a verse."

As the pages rustled over, her eyes rested on words which seemed to bounce off the page to meet her.

The Lord had answered her request. He had given her "a verse".

It was Ecclesiastes chapter 11 and verse 5.

Phyllis read these words, over and over again.

"As thou knowest not what is the way of the spirit, nor how the bones do grow in the womb of her that is with child: e'en so thou knowest not the works of God who maketh all."

That was it. Her verse. Her revelation from God.

Over the previous six years Phyllis had often been tempted to question the ways and works of God. This verse told her that she could never even attempt to know or understand His ways. But she could accept them as best.

This was a tremendous consolation.

The works of the God who had made everything were away beyond her knowledge.

Yet He knew about her. And cared for her as well.

Someday she would find out the reason for it all.

But not now. Not yet.

Some of the most trying times for Hertford and Phyllis in those early days of December were when Ford, aged four-and-a-half, told them how much he missed his brothers.

One evening, after they had eaten their meal, but before they left the table, he said, completely out of the blue, "I miss Thomas and Wendsley, but I know they are away to heaven."

After a short pause, which created a silence that could almost be touched, he asked about something which he had obviously been contemplating for some time.

"Will they be fixed when they come back?" he enquired.

In his childish mind he had imagined heaven to be some kind of celestial service centre where less-than-perfect-humans were repaired and then returned to their families.

It proved difficult for his loving, and grieving, parents, to explain to him tenderly that Thomas and Wendsley were already "fixed". They were with Jesus in heaven and had been changed.

But no. They wouldn't be coming back.

Hertford and Phyllis then told him how they expected to see their other two boys again in heaven, but this could only happen after they themselves had also died.

There were up days and down days for all three of them as time progressed.

For many people the bleak mid-winter is brightened by the coming of Christmas. Hertford and Phyllis used to love the excitement of those run-up-to-Christmas days.

This year they dreaded those days approaching.

During the third week of December, both parents decided that Ford would have a Christmas despite all that had happened.

They would buy him a good present.

He had told them both what he wanted. It was a car racing track set.

Although they found themselves unable to summon up any enthusiasm whatsoever for Christmas shopping, Hertford and Phyllis drove into Portadown and stopped outside a department store.

Phyllis went in and up the stairs. She knew exactly what she wanted.

Jingly Christmas music was playing, and the store floor was crowded with happy but harassed parents being lobbied by happy but insistent children.

An assistant asked Phyllis if he could "help her".

Phyllis enquired if they sold car racing track sets.

"Oh yes, we have a whole selection of them."

The assistant was being ever so helpful. "Which model is it that you want?"

Phyllis couldn't stay there a moment longer. Seeing all those children with their parents was just too much for her.

Muttering something about having "to see" she made for the stairs.

Hertford was waiting in the car outside.

"Have they not got them?" he asked, when Phyllis got into the passenger seat beside him, empty-handed.

"They have them O.K. in the place upstairs," she replied. "But I couldn't stick it in there. I had to come out. You may go in and get it."

Hertford did just that.

He went into the shop, up the stairs and bought the most suitable racing track he could see, in double quick time.

Returning to the car in less than ten minutes, much to his wife's surprise, for she knew how busy the shop was, Hertford opened the boot and tossed in a black bin bag.

That was Christmas for Ford all wrapped up for 1989.

Wrapped up in black.

The heartbroken parents couldn't ignore the memory of Thomas and Wendsley at Christmas either. Happy recollections of their glowing-at-Christmas-faces haunted sleepless nights. They wanted to buy something for them as well.

So on Christmas Eve they drove to Lisburn where they purchased two plain holly wreaths, draped with red ribbons.

On their way home they placed them on the simple double grave in Dromore.

That was Christmas for Thomas and Wendsley all wrapped up for 1989.

Wrapped up with a wreath.

CHAPTER TWENTY-EIGHT

Dead Leaves - New Life

✤✤✤

1990, the new year, began just as gloomily as the old one had ended.

Times were hard.

Days were short, and cold.

Nights were long.

Things were tough.

5th January would have been Thomas's birthday. He would have been six years old.

That afternoon the grieving parents removed the holly wreaths and placed six red roses on the grave in Dromore.

How could they ever forget?

When would they ever accept?

In mid-January Phyllis took a walk out around the bungalow one morning- just for something to do. Ford had just gone off to school. Hertford had been down in the chicken house for some time.

It was nine-thirty.

The previous night had been bitterly cold and hoar frost covered the ground. A dull off-white in the morning light.

Phyllis didn't notice the extreme cold. She was preoccupied. Totally absorbed in her own thoughts.

As she walked around the corner of the bungalow she looked across at the flower bed. She noted what had once been a clump of carnations. What had been a succession of glorious colour the previous summer was now a mound of drooping vegetation.

The grey-white spikes of the carnation leaves hung limp and lifeless, covered by frosty rime. Even the stalks seemed to have flopped out, given up. They lay black and brittle on the rock-hard soil.

Whether it was the pattern of the frost or the carnation leaves, or the effect of the frost on the carnation plant, something compelled Phyllis to walk over, bend down, and take a closer look.

Reaching forward, she lifted up a particularly sorry-for-itself looking stalk which lay at an angle to the main clump.

It broke off in her hand.

All of a sudden Thomas and Wendsley came before her in a vivid recollection. She could picture clearly in her mind the little faces that she used to put cream on. She could feel the delicate strands of the hair that she used to comb, time and time again.

Standing there in the winter garden, clutching a broken, lifeless carnation stalk, Phyllis was transfixed.

She felt she could almost smell her sons' fresh skin after they had been bathed.

Their hearty laughter rang in her ears. What she would have given at that moment just to have seen them again in the flesh. To have touched them. To have looked in to their happy faces …

Glancing down at the flower-bed again returned her to reality.

Different thoughts invaded the troubled mother's mind. Infinitely less pleasant ones.

"They are dead. In the soil. Brittle and decaying. Just like those plants. Once in bloom. Now dead and gone. They will turn to dust …"

Don't kid yourself, You will never hold them again ...

She recalled two dreadful days in November.

She went back to Dromore.

Back to the cemetery.

She heard the hollow thump of the soil on one little coffin. Then on another.

Warm tears overflowed on to cold cheeks.

Then the questioning began. Again.

"Why had all this to be?

Why did we have to lose both of them?"

Phyllis was overwhelmed with a mixture of anger and depression.

"Now we are in our new bungalow.

Now, at last we can cope financially.

And now they have been taken away from us ..."

Thus ran her thoughts.

Eventually realising that she was becoming stiff with cold, she dropped her limp carnation and walked round towards the back door.

Walking up the gentle ramp, especially designed for the boys' wheelchairs, she cried out in agony.

"Lord, please, please, don't let me think like this.

I don't want to think like this. Help me, Lord, to trust in You."

Despite her prayer, and despite her deliberate efforts to resign herself to what she knew to be the will of the Lord, Phyllis continued to be bombarded by unsettling thoughts for some days and months to come.

So too did Hertford. He tried to cope in a more silent, manly, fashion.

But it was hard. Very, very hard.

On a number of occasions during that lonely winter Hertford would come up from his work on the farm. A profound emptiness was creating an extreme restlessness in his spirit.

"Come on," he would say to Phyllis. "We will go over to Dromore."

Having stopped somewhere to buy flowers on the way, they would place two little bunches tenderly on the grave with the two little coffins in it.

Then they would sit there, wrapped up against the winter weather, and silently weeping, for half-an-hour. Sometimes an hour.

Visitors decreased in numbers as the days progressed.

Hertford and Phyllis kept up bravely when they were in, chatting to them. After all, it was more than two months now since the boys had passed away.

They didn't want people to consider them weak. Sickly sentimental.

Put your trust in God.

Look ahead, not back.

Face up to it fair and square.

Wasn't that what they were supposed to do?

That was what they were appearing to do while the well-wishers sat and talked.

The visitors hadn't reached the end of the lane on their way home, however, until Hertford and Phyllis had exploded in floods of tears.

They even went shopping away from their local stores. The weekend groceries were bought in Lisburn or Banbridge. It didn't matter to them where they went as long as the other people with the trolleys and the check-out operators were all strangers.

It was hard to retain composure, they found, when choosing their breakfast cereals, if some extremely well-meaning person would approach they and say "Hertford and Phyllis," or it could be "Mr and Mrs Arnold. I was awfully sorry to hear about your two wee boys ..."

Apart then from their trips to the graveyard in Dromore and short shopping forays to neural venues, most of their time was spent in and around the house.

Socialising of any sort had become a problem. Well-nigh an impossibility.

Hertford and Phyllis were finding the loss, the loneliness, the awful emptiness, the utter sense of futility, really painful.

In mid-April Phyllis took a walk around the bungalow again one morning.

It was spring. The daffodils had reappeared, yellow trumpets surrounded by green spears, to brighten the lane.

It was almost lunch-time, but still cool. As the despairing mother wandered slowly along, her eyes rested on the bunch of carnations whose frosted lifelessness had arrested her during the winter.

What a transformation!

Life had returned!

The grey spiky leaves were stiff and straight. On looking more closely she noticed that a few buds were beginning to swell at the ends of lengthening stalks.

Phyllis felt elated.

Desperation disappeared for an instant.

Closing her hands and raising her arms to God she exclaimed, "Praise the Lord! That's it!"

The sudden recollection of the realisation that Thomas and Wendsley would not just decay in the cold earth forever put a different complexion on things.

The God who could restore frosted, blackened carnation stalks to life would restore Thomas and Wendsley's bodies and change them too. "Fix them" for Ford.

Then when resurrected bodies were reunited with happy souls she and Hertford would rejoin them as well. To be forever with the Lord. And each other. In perfection and bliss.

Why then should she be depressed?

Thomas and Wendsley had never appeared to be depressed. They had never ever looked unhappy. They had just smiled and laughed and played for the most of their short lives.

Their parents could never have been any use to them while they were alive if they had been down in the dumps all the time. And they certainly weren't going to be any good to each other or anybody else if they were going to spend the remainder of their days just moping around.

There was the promise, and the prospect, of new life. They must be positive about the future, whatever it held.

When Hertford came into the kitchen, almost an hour later, for his lunch, Phyllis was bursting to tell him of her discovery.

"You remember back in January, Hertford," she began, "I told you about an experience I had out in the garden. When I saw the dead plants with frost all over them. How I was sickened and shocked when I thought that Thomas and Wendsley were just like those plants. Dead and gone. Disintegrating into the dust in the soil."

"Yes. I remember that," her husband replied. He remembered it well in fact, for neither of them had slept a wink for two nights after it.

"Well, I was out there again just before you came up," she continued, "and you will never believe it! The plant that was then just a big dead clump has now all perked up. In fact there are wee buds coming out on it again!"

"Yes, well isn't that the way plants go? They die off in the winter and then perk up again in the spring," Hertford replied. Obviously he hadn't grasped the deeper meaning of the illustration.

"That's true. It is," Phyllis concurred. "But can you not see what I'm getting at. I believe that God used it to teach us, well me anyway, a lesson. And it's this …

God can bring new life. He can make dead things live. Thomas and Wendsley aren't dead. Their souls are alive and one day He will give new life to their bodies and they will be recreated in heaven.

Our two little boys will be perfect!"

Phyllis paused to gauge her husband's reaction to this revelation. He sat gazing at her thoughtfully, idly tapping a teaspoon on the table.

She hadn't told him anything yet which he didn't already know. And which Phyllis herself should have already known also.

But it was the freshness with which it came that he warmed to. Phyllis had spoken with more enthusiasm than he had seen her display for anything for six months!

And she hadn't finished yet either.

There was more.

"I also believe that God has shown me that we should be more positive about things. Less depressed and moody.

God doesn't expect it. The boys would never have wanted it. So why don't we face the future. Do our best for God, for each other, for Ford and for everybody else that we can, trusting in Him to help us?"

Hertford continued pensive. He hadn't spoken yet on the matter.

It was right, he knew

It was sensible, he knew.

It would be tough, he knew.

"O.K." he agreed, at length. "We will do our best, as you say,"

They smiled bravely at each other.

God had spoken to them again.

This time through his creation.

CHAPTER TWENTY-NINE

Cottage Catering

✠ ✠ ✠

Not long after her God-in-the-garden revelation Phyllis said to her husband one day, "You know, Hertford, I am bored in the house. I can have all my housework done before you come up for your lunch and then I have far too much time on my hands. That gives me time to think. I want to be positive about our situation, but I really need something to keep me busy. All the time."

She had come to realise that unless she could occupy her mind with other things, memories of Thomas and Wendsley were going to dominate the thoughts of her waking hours, no matter how hard she tried to be forward-looking.

"Why don't we start back to making the trifles again?" Hertford replied, almost immediately.

He was all for doing his best to be more constructive in his outlook, but he could see that Phyllis was finding it tough.

There had been a number of times in the previous few months when he had considered suggesting that they get back to the trifle-making, even if it was only in a small way. It would give them both, but particularly Phyllis, something definite to do.

Rewarding, positive thinking for her at that particular time, was bound to prove an uphill journey, all the way. She needed help.

He had the broken heart of a father but with the chicken house to occupy his mind and energies.

Phyllis had the broken heart of a mother but with nothing to do other than housework, which she did mechanically. To her it was required, rather than rewarding, work.

So now Phyllis had expressed her problem so concisely, Hertford seized upon the opportunity to express his suggested solution.

"I was wondering about that too, Hertford," came the response, after a moment or two of reflection. "But maybe it's a bit soon yet. We will think about it for a wee while."

Their "wee while" that they had decided to leave to allow them to "think about it" turned out to be exactly that. A very short time. Just a couple of days.

One evening the phone rang.

It was a distributor to whom they had been supplying trifles in the busy days of the previous summer. His request was simple.

"Could you supply me again with the trifles we were selling last year?" he enquired. "I am constantly being asked for them."

It was arranged that he should call at their home on a Thursday evening to discuss the matter further.

Could this be a Heavenly confirmation of a Hertford suggestion?

When the distributor called that evening and told them of the constant enquiries that he had been receiving about the trifles, Hertford and Phyllis agreed to start supplying him again.

Here was something they could do.

Something which they KNEW they could do.

Something to keep both hands and minds occupied.

It was agreed that the first order would be delivered early in the following week.

This undertaking led to instant activity. It meant back to the planning. Back to the buying. Back to the Aga.

The Aga was the hard bit. And the first night was the hardest.

The smell of melting jelly in the kitchen seemed to highlight an emptiness in the house. There was nobody waiting for the leftover jelly. There would be nobody to get excited about some leftover cream.

As they stood there stirring, then pouring jelly, on the first-evening-back, tears flowed freely.

Happy memories flooded into active minds.

Hertford described his feelings to Phyllis at one stage.

"I know this is good for us. It is probably the best thing for us. But I feel as though I am walking over the boys' grave."

They were both experiencing a similar sensation.

It was as though the body was galloping ahead, proclaiming, "This is great. I'm glad to be occupied. Keep it up!"

All the time, however, the mind was holding each one of them back with the reins which had "Guilt" stamped all over them. These reins of guilt transmitted messages like "Think about the boys. How can you be so thoughtless, and appear so normal? You are letting them down. Neglecting their memory."

As they retired to bed on that first-back-to-the-jelly-and-custard-and-cream evening, Hertford and Phyllis felt sad, yet satisfied.

Their hearts were still sore, but their minds and hands had been restored to a former degree of usefulness.

How would the trifles take off this time?

Well, if their friend had gauged the situation accurately, there was obviously a demand.

They would see. Time would tell.

Again they didn't have long to wait.

The distributor had been right. There was a demand.

Orders began to roll in. And increase rapidly.

Soon a previous and familiar work pattern was re-established.

Phyllis saw Ford off to school and started to set up the trifles for the orders to be delivered that day. Hertford then came up from the chicken house, had a shower, donned the whites and did his bit, the packaging and delivery.

In a week's time they were on the phone with Heather, asking her to come over and help them again.

She readily agreed.

Now there were three of them.

Orders continued to roll in. The word had got around. "The wee trifles were back in the shops."

As they became busier day by day, Hertford and Phyllis came to realise that God had devised His own programme of occupational therapy for them.

They had learnt how to make and market trifles five months before Thomas and Wendsley had died.

God knew that He would be taking their little ones home to Himself. And He, in His wisdom, had arranged for something for them to do.

The grieving parents began gradually to appreciate that they weren't, "walking over their boys' graves," as they had at first imagined, but that they were, in fact, implementing God's plan for their lives.

As time went on and the summer progressed the busy couple were getting very little sleep. Long hours at work and short nights in bed became the order of each day.

They employed more staff.

Soon there were eight of them coming and going throughout the day. Making trifles, hundreds of them, in the bungalow. Things became rather cramped.

Throughout the increased activity of those summer days there were times when Hertford and Phyllis would suddenly remember the boys.

Something would arrest them abruptly. Stop them dead in their tracks.

It may have been the smell of melting jelly. It could have been a spoon, lying tilted at a crazy angle in a stainless steel bowl containing the remnants of some unscraped-out cream. It could have been the now empty doorway where Wendsley used to sit, propped up. Watching, waiting.

A seemingly inconsequential word, or action, or smell, or situation, could bring the tide of nostalgia flooding back.

They used to stop, as individuals, at such moments and thank God for the boys, and for their memory, and then proceed again with the job in hand.

And still the demand increased.

During the summer it became evident that in order to supply all the shops and supermarkets who were expressing an interest in stocking their product, a purpose-built factory unit would be required.

This meant sitting down with architects and advisors and drawing up plans for such a one-thousand-square-foot unit.

Hertford and Phyllis consoled themselves with the thought that when the new unit was complete life would become a little easier for them.

It didn't turn out that way.

The new purpose-built production unit was operational in four months, but in that period the market had increased apace.

Life now, even with increased staff and automated machinery, became even more frenetic.

In a short time the new unit proved to be too small to cope with the volume of business they were doing. Demand for new lines meant that not only were the original trifles being produced in ever increasing quantities, but now cheesecakes and puddings had been added as well.

The unit was doubled in size.

The staff was doubled in size.

There are presently twenty full-time members on the production staff. Outlets all over Ireland are being supplied. Plans are afoot for a new modern factory in Dromore, County Down.

Hertford and Phyllis were amazed at the rapid expansion of their business interests.

God had been so good to them.

One of the things that used to worry them in the earlier days was attending business meetings with high powered executives from some supermarket chain or other, in some shiny office somewhere.

They reckoned themselves to be just ordinary country people who lived down at the end of a big long lane in the absolute heart of nowhere.

What would they say?

They were by no means "posh" and they couldn't put it on.

Would the bossman understand them even?!

They needn't have worried. Time and time again they proved the wonderful grace of God.

The country couple were given words to say which they had never before used, and they were given an understanding of business principles which they never before even knew existed.

Unexpected doors opened without the slightest push.

When they placed their future in God's hands, they realised that the One who had taken to Himself their two little lambs, was still their loving Shepherd.

It was also exciting, but humbling, to prove practically the truth of the Saviour's own words from the sermon on the mount...

"But seek ye first the kingdom of God and his righteousness: and all these things shall be added unto you." Matthew 6 v. 33.

CHAPTER THIRTY

'This Is My Story'

✦✦✦

"This is my story, this is my song,
Praising my Saviour all the day long."
(Frances van Alstyne)

One day early in 1991 a Christian neighbour came into the factory where Hertford and Phyllis were working away. He had a proposal to put to them.

"I was wondering if either of you, or if both of you, would consider telling your story … 'Giving your testimony' if you like to call it that … in the wee Mission Hall up the road?" he asked.

The young couple looked at each other in silence. Here was something else they could do. Something more for God than themselves. They could "praise their Saviour" if they accepted this invitation.

When he had received an assuring nod from his wife, Hertford replied, "O.K. We will give it a go. Mind you we have never done it before, but I'm sure everybody has to start somewhere."

Their first meeting in that local Mission Hall with a very small congregation proved to be a nervous, stumbling start.

But there was warmth. There was feeling. There was God.

The encouraging comments from their friends and neighbours on the way out, helped them to appreciate how worthwhile it had been.

Hertford and Phyllis went home happy that evening. They felt on fire for the Lord. They had been able to stand up and witness to His saving, guiding and keeping power, in their own townland. Wonderful.

News travels fast in country parts. It wasn't long until they received their second invitation. Their first meeting had been on Hertford's home ground - Donacloney. Their second invitation was to speak in a Hall in the village where Phyllis had been brought up. Dollingstown.

This second meeting differed from the first only in the fact that the crowd was much bigger.

The hall was packed to capacity. In the end, a few latecomers ended up standing around the walls.

From the very moment when they began to speak Hertford and Phyllis felt an amazing sense of the presence of God.

As they related the step-by-step dealings of God through the traumas and triumphs of their lives, people were moved to tears.

Soon there wasn't a dry eye in the hall.

God was at work

Again, after the meeting, people told them of how the story had touched their hearts.

And again they felt that glow of satisfaction. That sense of having been able to return praise to God for his gracious guidance in their lives.

Very soon the lives of Hertford and Phyllis had taken on a second pattern.

This time, however, it wasn't a work pattern. It wasn't an early rising, jelly-melting, cream-spreading, tub-filling, van-driving pattern.

It was a witness pattern. It was a meeting-going, heart-searching, Christ-exalting, tear-producing pattern.

Hertford and Phyllis were soon being asked to testify in many places, all over Northern Ireland.

Usually someone would ring up and ask for Hertford or Phyllis. The caller would most likely, but not always, be from a church group.

"We have heard about you from Mrs. Blank in Ballymacsomething and we were wondering if you would be free to come and speak to our group? There are one or two people whom we think your story would help or encourage … We meet on a Tuesday night. You could have your pick of two dates - either the 14th March or the 11th April …" would be a typical request.

Hertford and Phyllis never refused an invitation if at all possible. They were afraid to.

If the God who meant so much to them had led somebody to ask them to the Backwoods Bible Church, well then, they would go.

Perhaps there would be someone there whom He had planned that they could help.

They have spoken to very large audiences, and to rather small ones. They have spoken in city churches and country halls.

And it has nearly always been their experience that there has been at least one grieving soul in the congregation to whom their testimony has been a help or an encouragement, or a hesitant heart to whom it has come as a challenge.

People have stood, silently weeping, holding tightly on to the hand of either of the speakers.

"That was great," they have sobbed. "That was a marvellous help to me. You see I lost a son, or a daughter, when he or she was three, or six, or nine … And I am still struggling to come to terms with it."

Others have written letters, phoned up, or even stopped Hertford or Phyllis on the street.

Every time that they hear of their testimony being blessed, Hertford and Phyllis give the praise to God.

This is their story - praising their Saviour - all the day - every day - long.

Though many people have declared themselves inspired by the testimony, the greatest help, encouragement and challenge or any evening is to the pair who testify themselves. Hertford and Phyllis.

It makes them feel so close to God. And to each other. And to Thomas and Wendsley.

Every testimony meeting brings the two boys back to life for an evening in their hearts. Often they drive to a meeting in tears, having been considering what they were going to say.

Occasionally their route to the meeting would take them past the cemetery in Dromore.

They would slow down and look over.

"Boys, we are away to talk about you tonight," one of them would say.

Then they would accelerate, wipe away a tear, and continue to the meeting.

That family bond, though broken for a while, is very evident when Hertford and Phyllis speak. It is this which allows suffering souls to identify with them.

Hertford often quotes the Scripture verse from Philippians ch. 1 "For to me to live is Christ. And to die is gain." v. 21.

"To me to live is Christ is why we are here tonight," he explains. "We want to tell you more about Him. "And to die is gain" That is what we are looking forward to. The gain that can only come to us after death. To meet the Lord, and Thomas and Wendsley again. They are now with the Lord. We are going to join them there. Isn't it marvellous to think that the first words that Thomas and Wendsley ever spoke were to the Saviour? And the first steps that they ever took were when they went to walk with Him."

Phyllis has never forgotten those who encouraged her through the most difficult of days. The most trying of experiences. She will always be grateful to them. How they pointed her back to God.

Thus when she speaks she likes to take the opportunity to succour those who are passing through testing times. Particularly those who are coping daily with the increased demands of a child or children with special needs.

She likes to remind them of the privilege that has been granted to them by God.

"If there is anyone here who is the father or mother, sister or brother, granny or granda, uncle or aunt, to a child with special needs, count that a privilege, she tells them tenderly. "He or she is extremely special, for he or she is a gift from God."

Hertford and Phyllis both live the message. They convey so tenderly the wealth of love that their two "gifts from God" brought to them in their short lives.

They often refer to Thomas and Wendsley as their "two little angels," because after the boys' death someone gave them a book of poems by Helen Steiner Rice.

Their favourite poem, the one which seemed to describe their life and experience so accurately was this:

BLESSINGS IN DISGUISE ARE DIFFICULT TO RECOGNISE

God sends His "little angels"
in many forms and guises,
They come as lovely miracles
that God alone devises -
For He does nothing without purpose
everything's a perfect plan
To fulfil in bounteous measure
all He ever promised man -
And every "little angel"
with a body bent and broken
Or a little mind retarded
or little words unspoken,
Is just God's way of trying

to reach and touch the hand
Of all who do not know Him
and cannot understand
That often through an angel
whose "wings will never fly"
The Lord is pointing out the way
to His eternal sky
Where there will be no handicaps
of body, soul or mind,
And where all limitations
will be dropped and left behind -
So accept these "little angels"
as gifts from God above
And thank Him for this lesson
in FAITH and HOPE and LOVE.

CHAPTER THIRTY-ONE

The Best News!

❖ ❖ ❖

"I have no mummy or daddy but I am not really worried about that. The Lord looks after me." Such was the testimony of an eleven-year old African boy.

In May 1994 Hertford and Phyllis took Ford along to hear the African Children's Choir in Ballynahinch, Co. Down.

One by one some of those young children with shining faces, told of their trust in God. Their faith vibrated and radiated as they sang.

It touched Ford's heart.

On the way home in the car he was very quiet. When they stopped at the front of the bungalow, Phyllis jumped out of the car at once. She ran round the back of it in time to speak to her husband before Ford got out.

"Say nothing, but Ford is crying in there," she whispered.

Just before bedtime Ford sat, legs tucked under him, in the rocking-chair in front of the Aga.

The chair gave an occasional squeak as he rocked to and fro, obviously deep in thought.

"Could we not bring some of those wee children here?" he asked at length. "They have no mummies or daddies and we have plenty of room."

Hertford and Phyllis didn't reply at once.

They couldn't. They were struck dumb. Rendered speechless.

Their by-now-only son was clearly upset.

Yet there was something more, something further, something deeper, on his mind.

"Mummy, I would love a wee brother," he blurted out finally, with a sob and a sigh.

His mummy knew how he felt. A silent tear tricked down her cheek.

He must be desperately lonely,.

But what could she say? How could she explain?

"Only God knows if He is going to give us any more children," she told him gently. "It is He who knows whether you will have another brother or not."

Later, after Ford had gone to bed, his parents sat up talking, far into the night.

"Isn't it an awful pity of Ford on his own?" Phyllis would ask repeatedly. She didn't need Hertford, or anybody else, for that matter, to give her the answer to her question.

Yes. 'Of course it was an awful pity of Ford on his own.' But what were the implications?

What would happen if they had another child and he or she turned out to be handicapped? And then died?

It had happened with two-thirds of their family so far.

Could they cope with that all again?

That night before she went to bed, Phyllis prayed.

That night as she tossed and turned sleeplessly in bed, Phyllis prayed.

For many nights and days to come, Phyllis prayed.

"Lord, if You want us to have another baby please reveal it to us. Only You can give us another child, and we want Your will to be done in our lives," was her simple prayer.

The summer passed quickly. It was very busy. Cottage Catering had become a household name and for five days every week Hertford and Phyllis rose early and retired late, just to keep abreast of demand.

Days became shorter. The warm days of summer made way for the crisp days of autumn.

Winter was approaching.

It was November, 1994.

Late one evening as the ever active couple tidied up around the kitchen, Phyllis shared a suspicion that she had, with her husband.

"I think I should tell you Hertford," she announced rather bluntly, "that I am nearly sure that I am pregnant again."

Hertford stopped what he was doing abruptly.

He turned, rested against the bench, and folded his arms.

No words came for a moment.

Then he retorted, incredulously. Gruffly too, it seemed to Phyllis, "Catch yourself on, ma, you couldn't be!"

"May be you think I couldn't be Hertford," his wife replied. She knew him only too well and had anticipated his reaction.

"May be you think I couldn't be," she echoed, "but I am almost certain that I am!"

Hertford was stunned.

He started to walk about. Short steps from here to there. And back. Like a fairground roundabout. Round and round. Up and down. Going nowhere.

He picked things up that didn't need to be picked up and set them down again where they didn't need to go.

"What are we going to do?" he kept asking. It was his turn to repeat a question.

"What ARE we going to do?"

The "what if? ..." doubts had begun to sneak in already, before the pregnancy had even been confirmed.

Then he decided that if Phyllis wasn't one hundred per cent convinced that she was right, then it was definitely time that they both knew for sure.

"Is there any way that you can be really certain? Find out for definite, I mean," he enquired.

He was a man of the soil. And the chicken house. And latterly of a factory full of trifles.

But he wasn't well up in matters gynaecological.

"Yes, I suppose there is," Phyllis volunteered. "I could have a scan."

"Well, arrange for a scan as soon as you can," Hertford instructed, his poetic turn of phrase occurring more by chance than by choice. "Then we will know."

Phyllis did as he requested and when the results of the scan were revealed they were positive.

It was true. Medically confirmed.

Phyllis was expecting another baby.

By that time, however, Hertford had recovered from the initial shock. He was glad for them, and for Ford. It must be, it had to be, the will of God.

Hertford and Phyllis hugged each other after they heard the result.

It was great. Another baby. A brother or sister for Ford. But what if ...?

They would have to tell Ford when a suitable opportunity presented itself. He would have to be the first to know, when the time was right ...

It was late one night and just shortly before Christmas that Hertford and Phyllis were sitting in bed chatting.

They knew that Ford, in his bedroom across the hall, wasn't asleep.

It seemed to be the ideal time to let him into the secret ...

"Ford, are you still awake?" Phyllis called.

"Yes. Why?" came the almost guilty response.

"Come in here a minute, we have something to tell you," his mum continued.

In two seconds their son was standing a t the end of their bed. Hair sticking out all over the place, eyes bright. Obviously sleep had been very far away.

"What is it?" he enquired breathlessly. All he could think of was his list of Christmas presents.

"Sit down on the end of the bed there, son," Hertford suggested. "Your mummy has good news for you."

"Good news. What is it mummy? Please tell me ..."

Eager expectation had taken over.

"What? Guess what? Go on, guess. What do you think it could be?" Phyllis thought that she would play the "guess what" game with him, that they often played when opening presents.

"Ach, mummy, stop keeping me going. I haven't a clue. What is it?" Ford was excited now but becoming impatient.

"Do you remember the night when we went to hear the African Children's Choir, away back in May?" Phyllis became serious as she began to explain. "Do you remember what you told us that night?"

"Yes, I do." Ford replied after only a moment's hesitation. "I said I would like a wee brother."

"That's right," his mum went on. Both she and his dad were amused at the quizzical look which had come over his face. "And I told you that only God knew if we were going to have another baby or not. Well, we ARE going to have another baby next year. You are going to have a little brother or sister!"

Ford sat motionless for a few seconds until the full impact of the message sank in. Then he jumped off the end of the bed and hugged his mummy, much to her surprise, for he had never been an emotionally demonstrative sort of child.

He was crying again. But it was for joy this time.

On releasing Phyllis from the bear hug, he took to running up and down the hall, darting in to his own bedroom, then his parents' room and on an occasional lap, the bathroom, all the while proclaiming at the top of his voice, "Oh mammy and daddy, that's the best news! The best news I ever heard! I'm going to have a wee brother."

He never seemed to figure at all on the possibility of a "wee sister"! That just didn't even merit a thought!

When he had worked off the initial euphoria and was visibly beginning 'to run out of steam' Phyllis spoke to him again.

"What we have told you tonight is still a secret, son. So don't you tell anybody in the meantime. What you can do though is pray to God that He will give us a healthy baby. Will you do that?"

"Yes, I will indeed," he promised, and made reluctantly towards his bedroom.

This time he stayed in it.

As the months ticked by, Hertford and Phyllis thought and talked and prayed much about the baby to come.

It had come as such a shock to them. After nine years they had thought they weren't going to have any more children.

Now this. Another one. A fourth.

Would he or she prove to be another blessing from the Lord, or a further test of their faith.

What if ...?

CHAPTER THIRTY-TWO

Matthew

✤✤✤

It was in the dead of winter. Early February.

One of those nights when it was cold and raw outside but warm and cosy where we were.

Inside. In my study.

Hertford and Phyllis had come to see me, to do some further research into this book.

As we started to talk I noticed that they seemed edgy a bit. Uneasy, restless. They had that we-have-something-to-say-but-don't-know-how-to-say-it look about them. This was unusual. Normally we had an open, friendly, trusting relationship.

Eventually Phyllis 'broke the ice'.

"Do you remember, Noel, you told us a while ago to think of a last chapter for the book?" she began. "You said that you would like it to end on a high point. 'With a bang, and not with a whimper' was how you put it to us."

"Yes, I do. I remember," I replied. Finding where to end a biography is like finding where to start it. Hard sometimes.

"Well, we believe that we have the last chapter for you now," she went on rather sheepishly.

"That's good. Where do you think we should end?" I enquired.

"Didn't you say that you would like to have it finished by June?" Phyllis parried my question by asking one of her own.

"That's right," I had to agree, "Yes, I did say that."

"We have news then that should make the last chapter of the book no problem You see we are expecting another baby in June."

There was an awkward silence for a moment.

This would take some thinking about. But I didn't have a lot of time to think. My two friends were sitting directly opposite me. Awaiting my reaction.

"That is some news!" I began, not very sure of just how to respond. "I must admit that I am a bit shocked ..."

"'A bit shocked' are you?!" Hertford retorted. "I will tell you this, you're not half as shocked as I was!"

Then he smiled.

Looking over to where I was sitting, pen poised, he quipped, "Noel, can you spell 'numb'?"

There followed an animated conversation, when Hertford and Phyllis, relieved that I now knew their 'secret', shared with me how they felt about their fourth-child-to-come.

"We believe that this is the hand of God," Phyllis stated. "This is God's way of showing His approval for this book project. And His timing is just spot on."

"Yes," Hertford added, "Whatever happens, you will definitely have an end for the book."

The 'whatever happens' was the 'what if' of earlier days.

Spring with its daffodils in the lane, and lambs in the fields, seemed to hasten past, unnoticed.

Hertford and Phyllis were still very busy and every spare moment was spent in thinking about and planning for the new baby.

It wasn't long until their 'secret' could be 'kept a secret' no more.

Mums and dads were the first to be told the good news. Then other close relatives were informed. When the news was released to their wider circle of acquaintances the whole countryside was abuzz with it.

Friends speaking to Hertford and Phyllis said outwardly that it was 'great', and hoped inwardly that they wouldn't be heartbroken again.

The parents-to-be prayed much during those days. And praying was difficult.

"Lord, we want Your will to be done in our lives," they would begin. "We know that this new baby is from Yourself ..." Then the temptation was always to add, "And please, please God let him or her be normal ..."

June came. All would be revealed in a matter of days.

'What if?' would soon become 'What now?'

On the thirteenth of the month at 10:20 am the new baby arrived.

A boy. Six pounds and half-an-ounce. Red hair just like his dad ...

What a relief! At least he had arrived safely!

Then there was the anxious wait while tests were carried out.

It didn't take long, and the results were marvellous. The doctors in the hospital assured Hertford and Phyllis that their fourth son was a perfectly normal and healthy baby boy!

What excitement! What praise!

What a wonderful, caring God!

Phyllis was absolutely drained, and absolutely delighted.

Ford was absolutely ecstatic, and absolutely excited.

Hertford was just a wonderful mixture of every pleasant emotion known to man.

Soon the flowers, and presents, and cards began to arrive at the hospital.

Soon the friends began to arrive at the hospital.

The delighted grandparents of the new baby appeared, followed by his aunts and uncles and cousins galore. Then interested well wishers from near and far showed up to meet the latest addition to the Arnold family.

"And what are you going to call him?" they would all invariably ask, as they admired the miniature perfection of his little hands and feet, his tiny fingers and toes.

The baby yawned and stretched and slept and ignored everybody!

"We are going to call him 'Matthew," his happy parents were pleased to inform all enquirers. "We have chosen this name because 'Matthew' means 'a gift from God'. And that is what he is to us. Our gift from God."

On Sunday, 18th June, 1995, Hertford and Ford arrived at the hospital to bring Phyllis and Matthew home.

They made a number of car-to-ward-and-return journeys until they had all the flowers and presents safely packed into the car.

Then came the big moment. The four of them were united as a happy family, driving home.

On arrival at their bungalow Phyllis sat in the car with baby Matthew. Dad and big brother carried the presents, flowers and cards into the house and left them in what had once been Thomas and Wendsley's room.

Then Phyllis gently carried their new baby, their fourth son, into the bungalow and laid him in a pram in that room.

The rainbows and clouds, balloons and teddies, surrounded him.

It had been Thomas and Wendsley's room once.

But God had other plans for it.

It is Matthew's room now.

Their latest 'gift from God.'